Beautiful Hearted
WOMEN
of the BIBLE

A Creative
Mother-Daughter
Devotional

LINSEY DRISKILL

FOCUS
ON THE FAMILY.

A Focus on the Family Resource
Published by Tyndale House Publishers

I dedicate this book to my children,

Bates, Brooklyn, and Gracie,

the inspiration behind this dream—

may you always love the Lord and others

with all your hearts.

Table of Contents

Introduction

$\mathcal{A}$s my daughters were curled up in bed one night, reading princess books and wanting to dress up like them, a dream surfaced in my heart and mind.

What if my daughters wanted to imitate women in the Bible who loved God and others?

What if there was a devotional through which my daughters and your daughters could learn about women who changed the world? And what if they were inspired to imitate those women?

What if our daughters saw the freedom in caring more about inner beauty than outward beauty?

What if they saw that humility was the way to true beauty?

What if they grew in confidence as they learned to depend on the Lord?

What if we slowed down and took time to connect with our daughters?

What if a foundation could be built in our daughters' hearts, minds, and souls, to love Jesus with all their hearts and to love one another with the kind of love that expands God's Kingdom?

This book, *Beautiful Hearted Women of the Bible: A Creative Mother-Daughter Devotional*, is my answer to all of those what-if questions.

The Bible women in this book are beautiful hearted because they loved the Lord and others. They were moms and daughters just like we are. And they made mistakes and had areas to work on just like we do. But the examples of their lives, as recorded in Scripture, can serve to strengthen our faith and point us to the One who is perfect and has the power to forgive: Jesus.

Building Relationship . . . and Faith!

While one of our greatest desires as mothers is to be close to our daughters, it's easy to get swept up in technology and busyness and miss the chance to connect. This devotional offers a sweet space to slow down, be present, and interact with each other, so that relationship with the Lord and one another can supersede all else.

As the mother of triplets and a former teacher, I have learned that questions are a powerful way to engage children—not just to ensure they're paying attention and comprehending, but also to tap into their imaginations and hearts so we can learn more of who they are. Reflective and imaginative questions *within* each story help us do this. The questions should not be rushed, as they provide a window into our daughters' souls if we really listen to their answers.

The reflective questions within the stories help us to avoid teaching *at* our daughters, and instead encourage us to learn *with* them. Jesus asked about eighty questions just in the book of Luke, many times leading people to truth through reflection, so that is also my approach in this devotional.

This devotional helps build a strong faith foundation in our daughters' hearts, minds, and souls, while they're still coming to us for answers.

Devotional Components

Before each story, there is a verse called *Words for Your Heart* that can be reflected upon or memorized. You may want to write the verses on note cards, punch a hole in each corner, and then put them on a key ring for easy reference. A fun way to memorize Scripture is to create melodies and hand gestures to go with the words.

Stories of beautiful hearted Bible women follow each verse. Reflective and imaginative questions *within* each story foster connection and engagement. Following each story are three questions and a prayer.

The *Daughters in Action* section provides practical ways to put faith into action.

The *Creative Fun* section brings life and fun to our faith and relationships with the Lord and our daughters.

My kids and I have had so much fun doing all the activities together, and they have helped the truths of Jesus take root in their hearts.

Age for the Devotional

The devotional is written with six- to ten-year-old girls in mind; however, girls younger and older can also enjoy the lessons and activities and grow from them. Because of the reflective and imaginative questions, this devotional reaches a wide range of ages. Deep within, God has given us the ability to imagine, reflect, and uncover new truths about Him each day, so we can all grow from this devotional.

Some parts of the Bible are too advanced or too mature for young girls. Corrie ten Boom, in her famous book *The Hiding Place*, remembers a time when her father asked her to carry his heavy suitcase. "It's too heavy," she said. He replied, "Yes, and it would be a pretty poor father who would ask a little girl to carry such a load. It's the same way, Corrie, with knowledge. Some knowledge is too heavy for children. When you are older and stronger you can bear it."

The devotions in *Beautiful Hearted Women of the Bible* are written at a young girl's level so she is not given knowledge too heavy to bear.

How to Use the Devotional

Doing one devotion each week works well. This allows time to complete the activities without being rushed.

Each story takes about ten to fifteen minutes. The story time is intended to be done one-on-one—Mom and one daughter at a time. The connection you gain from having special time with one child, as well as hearing her answers to the questions without being influenced by a sibling, is powerful.

That being said, I know as moms our days are busy, so if you have multiple children, do what works for you.

Regarding the activities, I did some of them one-on-one, but most of the activities I did with all my kids at the same time.

If you choose to just read the stories and not do the activities, you could do one devotion reading each day. You can pick and choose some of the activities or complete all of them—whatever works for you.

However, the activities inspire connection with our daughters and help the truth from the Bible take root and settle into our children's (and our) hearts. They're also a lot of fun!

I am filled with joy as I imagine this devotional in your hands as you connect with your daughter. May the Lord work in both your hearts as you seek Him together. I pray that this devotional would inspire you to draw close to Jesus and each other and to follow the Lord's two greatest commandments: to love God and others.

With love,
Linsey

1

LOYAL TO
THE PROMISE—SARAI

(Genesis 12, 15)

Words for Your Heart

Trust in the LORD with all your heart,
and do not rely on your own understanding.

PROVERBS 3:5

Sarai was married to a man named Abram. They lived in a place called Haran. When Abram was seventy-five years old, God told him and Sarai to leave their home and move to a new place.

God didn't tell them where they were going, but He promised to show them the way. When God said it was time to move, Abram and Sarai trusted God and did just what He said. Sarai showed loyalty to her husband, Abram, by staying by his side throughout the long journey to the new land. *If you could move anywhere in the world, where would you want to go?*

Sarai and Abram were old—old enough to be grandparents. But they had no children.

Quite some time after they moved from their homeland, God appeared to Abram. God promised that Abram and Sarai would have a son even though they were too old to have children.

7

The Lord took Abram outside and said, "Look at the sky and count the stars." He then told Abram that he and Sarai would have as many descendants as stars in the sky. Descendants are the children, grandchildren, and so on, who would come after them. *So how many descendants did God promise them?* As many as the stars in the sky—that's a whole lot!

If you look at the sky on a dark night, you'll see many, many stars. But the Bible tells us that God knows every star in the sky, decides how many there will be, and even has a name for each star! (Psalm 147:4). *What does that tell you about God? If you could name a star, what would you name it?*

Every night, the stars in the sky were a reminder to Sarai and Abram of God's promise to them and His faithfulness. The stars were also a reminder for Abram and Sarai to remain loyal to the Lord and to each other as they remembered the promises to come.

However, God's promise didn't happen right away. Sarai and Abram waited, but there was still no baby. Sarai became jealous of a woman named Hagar who could have children. Imagine all your friends getting what they want, except you—well, that's what happened to Sarai. Sarai was so jealous that she mistreated Hagar. *If you hurt someone's feelings or mistreat someone, how can you try to work it out?*

Despite Sarai's imperfections, the Lord was with her and showed her grace. The Lord is also with you when you do well and when you make mistakes. *Do you think God forgot His promise to give Abram and Sarai a child just because Sarai made wrong choices?* No! God always keeps His promises.

Just as it was probably difficult for Sarai to believe in God's promise that she would have a child, it can also be hard for us to have faith when things don't happen right away. Sarai was learning to trust God more and more. Proverbs 3:5 tells us to trust in the Lord with all our hearts, even when we don't understand everything. We'll find out more about Sarai and Abram in the next devotion. *Can you guess what happened?*

? QUESTIONS

- How did Sarai show loyalty to Abram and to God?
- How can you be loyal to your friends and family?
- What is beautiful about Sarai's heart?

✝ PRAYER

Lord, help us to be loyal as Sarai was, and help us trust You when we don't understand everything. In Jesus' name, amen.

DAUGHTERS IN ACTION

A trust fall shows the importance of trust. Stand behind your daughter and extend your arms toward her. Call out, "Trust me!" and encourage your daughter to fall backward into your arms. Make sure to catch her! Discuss how people will trust us when we are dependable and loyal.

 CREATIVE FUN

Materials: A pan with raised edges, various food items

Create an edible model of the land Abram and Sarai traveled. Look up the Bible story in Genesis 12 and consult a map in the back of your Bible or online. Together with your daughter, brainstorm food items to represent water, land forms, and trees. For example, for water you could use blue licorice. Other ideas might include graham crackers for the land with squirts of chocolate syrup for mud, green sprinkles for grass, cupcakes with green icing for hills, and green lollipops for trees (you can use marshmallows to help them stand up). Let your imaginations come alive. Then enjoy eating your delicious creation!

2

GOD'S GREAT
GRACE—SARAH

(Genesis 17–18, 21)

Words for Your Heart

If we confess our sins, He is faithful and
righteous to forgive us our sins.

I JOHN I:9

Do you remember what Abram and Sarai were waiting for? God had promised that they would have a son.

One day, God appeared to Abram. It was getting closer to the time when the promise would be fulfilled. At this time, Abram was ninety-nine years old. And Sarai was ninety years old.

God said that Sarai's name was to change to Sarah, meaning "princess." God changed Abram's name to Abraham, meaning "father of many." *Do you know what your name means?*

God told Abraham that very soon Sarah would have a son.

Abraham fell facedown and laughed. He said, "I'm one hundred years old. Will I have a son now? Will Sarah have a child at ninety years old?"

God said again, "Your wife Sarah will have a son, and you will call him Isaac."

After that, God went up from him, and Abraham followed God.

A short time later, Abraham saw three visitors outside their tent. He went to get them milk, cheese, and meat, and Sarah baked bread for them. The visitors then told Abraham that Sarah would have a son this time next year. *How do you think the visitors knew when God's promise would be fulfilled?*

Sarah was inside the tent. She overheard what the men said and laughed to herself. Because she was old and past the normal age to have children, she didn't think it was possible.

The Lord then asked Abraham, "Why did Sarah laugh? Is anything too hard for the LORD?"

Sarah was afraid, so she lied and said, "I did not laugh."

But the Lord said, "Yes, you did laugh." *How do you think God felt when Sarah lied?* Proverbs 12:22 says that God hates lying, but He delights in those who keep their promises and are trustworthy. God wants us to be honest with Him and share what's really on our hearts. *What is another reason not to lie—how does it affect others?*

After Sarah lied, do you think God kept His promise that she would have a baby boy? Yes! The Lord always keeps His promises. God showed Sarah grace and mercy. He loved her despite the wrong choices she made. When you make a wrong choice, you can talk to the Lord about it. He sees through your hurts to your heart, and His love for you never changes. *In what area do you think you need help from the Lord?*

Getting things right the first time isn't what makes a person beautiful. Trying to love God and others with all our hearts is what makes a person beautiful. When we believe in Jesus, the Son of God, our sins are forgiven because of His great grace.

Just as the Lord promised, Sarah soon had a son named Isaac. Some of her descendants even became kings. Some of these kings were David, Solomon, and the greatest King there ever was . . . Jesus!

Even though Sarah struggled at times, she looked to God and grew in her faith. Hebrews 11:11 says that Sarah was able to have a baby because through faith, she believed that God would be faithful to keep His promise. God was gracious to Sarah and brought goodness from her life, and He can do the same for you.

After having Isaac, Sarah smiled and said, "God has brought me laughter. . . . Who would've thought that I'd have a child in my old age? Yet I have a son."

? QUESTIONS
- Why is being honest an important part of relationships?
- Based on Hebrews 11:11, how did Sarah grow in her faith?
- What is beautiful about Sarah's heart?

✝ PRAYER
Lord, we know that, like Sarah, sometimes we do things that are wrong. Please forgive us. Thank You for Your grace and for always keeping Your promises. Help us grow in our faith as Sarah did. In Jesus' name, amen.

▷ DAUGHTERS IN ACTION
Materials: Dominoes or tall blocks

Together, set up a long row of dominoes or tall blocks. Stand the dominoes close together so that when you knock the first one down, each domino will knock the next one over. Explain to your daughter that this shows how telling one lie can usually lead to telling more lies. Then discuss how the opposite is also true: When you tell the truth, it becomes easier to tell the truth. Have fun together trying to make more complex paths for the dominoes.

CREATIVE FUN

Materials: towel, disposable pan, 1 cup water, 2 cups cornstarch, strainer

Make oobleck with your daughter to illustrate that even when we make wrong choices, God is ready to forgive us.

1. Lay a towel under a disposable pan for easy cleanup.

2. Mix the water and cornstarch in the pan. At first the mixture will seem stiff, but when your hands touch the oobleck, it will loosen up. Add a teaspoon of water at a time to loosen it up more if it's too stiff. You can add some food coloring or washable paint to create more colorful oobleck.

3. Hold the strainer OVER the pan.

4. Fill a cup with oobleck and slowly pour it into the strainer. What happens to the oobleck? It flows through the holes of the strainer into the pan.

Explain that the oobleck represents people, the holes in the strainer represent the sins people commit, and the pan represents God's grace.

Tell your daughter that when we do wrong things and fall (just as the oobleck fell through the holes), God is there with His great forgiveness and grace. Discuss how God's grace "catches" us when we fall.

3

COURAGE AND COMPASSION— JOCHEBED, SHIPHRAH, PUAH, AND PHARAOH'S DAUGHTER

(Exodus 1–2)

Words for Your Heart

Stand firm in the faith; be courageous;

be strong. Do everything in love.

I CORINTHIANS 16:13-14, NIV

A long time ago, God's people, the Israelites, were slaves in Egypt. They had hard lives and were forced to do very difficult work. The king, also called Pharaoh, decided there were too many Israelites in his land, so he wanted to get rid of all the baby boys at once!

During that time, Shiphrah and Puah were Hebrew midwives. That meant they helped moms when it was time for them to have their babies. The cruel Pharaoh ordered the two midwives to get rid of all the baby boys, but to keep the baby girls.

But Puah and Shiphrah feared and loved God. They knew that what Pharaoh wanted them to do was wrong, and they had compassion for the babies. *What do you think they did?* They saved every baby boy born! God was pleased that they chose to do the right thing, and He showed them kindness.

But Pharaoh continued being cruel and ordering all the people to get rid of the baby boys.

There was an Israelite woman named Jochebed (jok-uh-bed) who had a baby boy. She lived in Egypt and was terrified of what might happen to her son. Jochebed was desperate to protect him, and she was afraid that the baby's crying would be heard—she had to find a way to save him.

Jochebed found a basket made of papyrus and coated it with tar so that it would float. She laid her baby inside and placed the basket in the reeds, or tall plants, by the Nile River. Because the reeds grew very tall, Jochebed was able to hide him well. Miriam, the baby's sister, stood at a distance, keeping an eye on her baby brother.

As Miriam watched him, she saw the daughter of Pharaoh, who was the princess, walk to the river to bathe.

Pharaoh's daughter saw the basket floating on the water and sent her helper to get the basket out of the river.

Miriam watched as the princess approached the baby, wondering what would happen. *How do you think Miriam was feeling in that moment?*

When Pharaoh's daughter saw the baby boy crying, she felt sorry for him. But she also knew her father, the cruel Pharaoh, had ordered all the baby boys to be gone at once. *What do you think she did?*

The princess was a hero that day because she saved the baby. Later the princess named him Moses.

When Moses grew up, he became a great leader for the Lord. Moses had the opportunity to be a great leader because these women chose to be courageous and save him.

? QUESTIONS

- What quality do Jochebed, Puah, Shiphrah, and Pharaoh's daughter all have in common?

- When was a time you were compassionate to someone or were courageous?
- What is beautiful about these women's hearts?

 PRAYER

Lord, help us to have courage and obey You first as Jochebed, Puah, and Shiphrah did. Help us to show compassion for others as Pharaoh's daughter did. In Jesus' name, amen.

 DAUGHTERS IN ACTION

The women in this Bible passage had compassion for others and the courage to do the right thing. Follow their example by either having courage to do something you've been afraid of doing or by showing compassion to someone who is struggling. For example, you could make a card for a sick friend or help a family in need.

 CREATIVE FUN

Materials: Chalk, a small rock

Play hopscotch together to help you memorize 1 Corinthians 16:13-14 (NIV) and to remember to be courageous and compassionate. Outside, use chalk to draw the hopscotch grid shown on the next page.

To play, toss a marker—such as a rock, stick, or beanbag—into the first square. If it lands outside the square, you lose your turn.

If the marker lands in square 1, say the word in that space, but hop over it, land on square 2, and also say the word there.

Continue hopping and saying the words all the way to square 10.

Then turn around and hop back. (Don't say the verse on the way back because it would be really hard to say backward!)

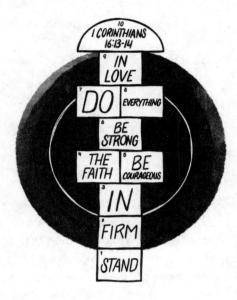

Pick up your marker on the way back without stepping in the square or falling.

Then the next person takes her turn.

When it's your turn again, throw your marker in square 2 and start there.

During your turn, if you do fall or step in the square that holds your marker, it's the next person's turn. Then, on your next turn, you must toss the marker into the same square again.

Whoever reaches square 10 first wins!

4

PRAISING GOD
—MIRIAM

(Exodus 3–15)

Words for Your Heart

The LORD is my strength and my shield;
my heart trusts in Him, and I am helped.
Therefore my heart rejoices,
and I praise Him with my song.

PSALM 28:7

*T*ime passed and Moses grew up. The Israelites were still slaves in Egypt and were treated very poorly. One day God said to Moses, "My people are suffering. I have seen them, and I have heard their cries. I am sending you to rescue my people out of Egypt." *What does that tell you about God?*

Moses wasn't sure that he could stand up to the evil Pharaoh. Moses asked, "Who am I to go to Pharaoh?" Moses wasn't sure that Pharaoh would listen to him.

God didn't answer Moses by telling him he could do it because of his great strengths. God just said, "I will be with you."

Then God said, "Tell the people that the LORD has sent you." God gave Moses several miraculous signs to help everyone know that He had truly sent Moses.

Then Moses said, "But God, I'm not a very good speaker. Words don't come easily to me. Please send someone else."

God said, "I will send your brother, Aaron, to help you. He is a good speaker. Also, I will help you and teach you what to say and do."

Moses and his brother, Aaron, went to Pharaoh and said, "God says, 'Let my people go.'" *Do you think Pharaoh let the people go?* Pharaoh refused, so God sent terrible plagues to the Egyptians. But Pharaoh still wouldn't let the Israelites leave. By the tenth awful plague, Pharaoh finally agreed to let the Israelites go.

Moses and Aaron led the Israelites to the sea. But Pharaoh soon regretted his decision and charged after them with chariots and horses. The Israelites were by the sea with nowhere to go. They were terrified and cried out to the Lord.

Moses said to the people, "The LORD will fight for you; just be still." Moses raised his staff and stretched his hand over the water. God used a strong wind to lift the waters on both sides to create a dry path!

The Israelites crossed the Red Sea on dry ground. When they were safe on the other side, the waters fell, wiping out the Egyptians.

Moses and Aaron had an older sister named Miriam. She was the one who had watched over Moses when he was a baby in the river. Miriam was a prophetess, which meant God revealed things to her.

To celebrate the great miracle the Lord did that day, Miriam picked up a tambourine to make music for the Lord. *What instrument would you have wanted to play if you were there?* Miriam led the Israelite women in singing and dancing to praise God. Miriam sang:

> *"Sing to the LORD,*
> *for He is victorious.*

He has thrown both
Horse and rider into the sea."

How do you think God felt as He watched these women praise Him? What a beautiful sound of celebration that must have been to the Lord.

It would have been easy to forget to take time to thank the Lord for His goodness, but Miriam gave credit to God for their victory. And many women followed her example in praising the Lord.

 ## QUESTIONS
- What is something you can praise God for?
- How can we be a good example in giving praise to the Lord?
- What is beautiful about Miriam's heart?

 ## PRAYER
Lord, help us to be great leaders for You and to praise and celebrate You as Miriam did. In Jesus' name, amen.

 ## DAUGHTERS IN ACTION
Create a poem or song together to praise the Lord like Miriam did. You can use a song or tune you already know and write new words for it. Take it a step further and make up some dance moves to go with the praise song or poem!

 ## CREATIVE FUN
Materials: Party supplies

Just as Miriam led the women in singing and dancing, plan a fun mother-daughter dance party to praise the Lord! Plan what food to have and what decorations to hang (such as Christmas lights or streamers), and create a list of praise songs to play. You can also read the poem or sing and dance to the song you made up in the Daughters in Action section.

5

STANDING UP FOR WHAT'S RIGHT—THE FIVE SISTERS

(Numbers 27)

Words for Your Heart

He has told you what is good and what it is the LORD requires of you: to act justly, to love faithfulness, and to walk humbly with your God.

MICAH 6:8

$\mathcal{T}$ry to say these five sisters' names three times fast: Mahlah, Noah, Hoglah, Milcah, and Tirzah. Tough, isn't it? The five sisters didn't have any brothers, so they must have had a lot of girl time! *They didn't have TVs, computers, phones, or other electronics back then, so what do you think they did with their time?* They probably spent a lot of time doing chores and coming up with games to play. *What's a family activity or game you like to play that doesn't need electricity?*

The time had come to divide up the land promised by God to the Israelites. Even though the five sisters and the rest of the Israelites had not yet seen the land, they believed God would give it to them. They showed what it means to have faith.

The father of the five sisters had died. In those days, when someone's dad passed away, his land was only left to sons, not daughters. But remember, there were no sons in the family to inherit the father's land. *So what do you think would happen to the land intended for their dad?* It would have been taken from them. *Can you imagine if your family bought a new house, and you were on your way to move in, but then found out it had been taken from you, and you had nowhere to go?* That's similar to what happened to the five sisters. *How do you think the sisters felt?*

The five sisters thought it was unfair that the land promised to their family would be taken away. They decided they needed to go to the leaders and ask them to make a change so that the law would be fair.

Together the five sisters approached the Tent of Meeting, which was a place the leaders discussed important matters and also where they met with God. The Tent of Meeting was similar to a church.

It was a big deal for the five sisters to stand up for themselves and try to change the law so they could have their land. The sisters might have been nervous, but they still had courage.

Do you remember Moses? He was one of the people leading the Israelites to the Promised Land, and he was a leader at the Tent of Meeting. The five sisters talked to the leaders and the whole assembly and said, "Our father's land shouldn't be taken away from our family just because he didn't have a son. Give us our father's land."

The sisters could have been rude to the leaders since the law was unfair, but instead they spoke respectfully to them.

Moses listened carefully, and then he talked to the Lord about it. *How do you think God responded to their plea to keep the land?* The Lord spoke to Moses and said, "What the sisters are saying is right. You must give their father's land to them."

The Lord is full of compassion. He is fair and kind in all He does. The sisters saw the goodness of God that day. *How do you think they celebrated this great news from God?*

 **QUESTIONS**
- How did the sisters honor God?
- Just as the five sisters spoke up for what was right, when have you stood up for someone or chosen to do the right thing?
- What is beautiful about the five sisters' hearts?

 PRAYER

Lord, help us to have faith in You and to have courage to stand up for what's right like the five sisters did. We praise You for showing compassion to them. Thank You for always listening to us. We know we can talk to You anytime, anywhere. In Jesus' name, amen.

 DAUGHTERS IN ACTION

Together, discuss times when you've witnessed someone being treated meanly or unfairly. What did you do? Talk about what you can do in the future if you see someone treated badly. What practical things can you do to stand up for that person and show kindness? Remember that you might be the only one who does.

 CREATIVE FUN

Your daughter can practice being a leader by making an obstacle course and leading you through it. If she is old enough, you may want her to complete a ropes course to build confidence in leading. Being a leader in small moments will prepare her to be a leader in bigger ones.

6

THE HIDING PLACE IN
A WALL—RAHAB

(Joshua 1–2)

Words for Your Heart

Haven't I commanded you: be strong and courageous?
Do not be afraid or discouraged, for the LORD
your God is with you wherever you go.

JOSHUA 1:9

*A*fter Moses died, Joshua continued leading the Israelites to the land God had promised them. They had been wandering in the desert for a long time. It was hot, dry, and dusty. There wasn't much water for them to drink, and there wasn't much grass for their animals to eat. It was a hard life.

But the Promised Land was described as flowing with milk and honey. That meant it had everything they could possibly need. There would be plenty of water and food for themselves and their animals. Life in the Promised Land would be pleasant and sweet. *What would your dreamland be like?*

Now it was time to cross the Jordan River and enter the Promised Land. Joshua would need to lead the Israelites in overtaking Jericho. The Lord had given Joshua strong leadership skills. *Just as Joshua was good at being a leader, what is something you're good at?*

The Lord said to Joshua, "As I was with Moses, so I will be with you. I will not leave you or forsake you. Haven't I commanded you: be strong and courageous? Do not be afraid or discouraged, for the LORD your God is with you wherever you go." *Why do you think the Lord said these words to Joshua?*

Joshua sent two Israelite men to spy on Jericho so they could discover the best way to conquer the city.

A woman named Rahab had the perfect lookout—her home was inside the wall that surrounded the city. *If your house could be in a wall like Rahab's, or in a tree, or have slides instead of stairs, or designed any way you could imagine, what would it be like?*

Rahab had lived a hard life. She had made many sinful choices. And she was a citizen of Jericho, where the people followed other gods rather than the Lord. But the spies needed her help.

The men made their way to Rahab's house. Rahab had to choose whether to protect her city or to help the two men Joshua had sent. If Rahab let the spies into her home and the king of Jericho found out, she would be in a lot of trouble. *What do you think she did?*

Rahab chose to be courageous. She let these men who followed God use her home as a lookout.

The king of Jericho heard the spies were there. He sent messengers to Rahab's home right away. Rahab quickly hid the men on the roof under the flax plants that were scattered there.

The king's men pounded on the door. Boom! Boom! Boom! Rahab scrambled to the door, but before opening it, she had to figure out what to do next! *Do you think she continued protecting the two Israelite men who followed God or said they were hiding on the roof?* We'll see in the next devotion!

QUESTIONS

- How did Rahab show courage?
- Why do you think Rahab helped the two spies?
- What is beautiful about Rahab's heart?

PRAYER

God, we are thankful that Rahab had courage to help Your followers. Please give us courage too. We want to follow You boldly with our words and our actions. In Jesus' name, amen.

DAUGHTERS IN ACTION

Materials: Kid-friendly cross-stitch kit

Find a kids' cross-stitch kit to use together. Explain to your daughter that when she keeps doing one stitch at a time, the project will eventually be completed.

When it's finished, show your daughter the back of the project—it looks messy just like life does at times. But when the project is turned over to the right side, it shows a beautiful picture.

Discuss this truth with your daughter: Even when life looked messy and scary for Rahab, she had courage and did the next thing she knew to do to help the men who followed God. You and your daughter can also be courageous by taking the next step to honor God.

CREATIVE FUN

Materials: Boxes, paper towel tubes, paint, other decorative items

Joshua was leading the Israelites to the Promised Land, which was a dreamland in many ways. Draw or create a model of what your dreamland or dream house would look like using boxes, paper towel tubes, paint, and other materials. As an alternative, you could draw it on cardstock or make it out of play dough. Have fun tapping into your imagination!

7

PROMISES FULFILLED
—RAHAB

(Joshua 2, 6)

Words for Your Heart

The LORD is trustworthy in all he promises
and faithful in all he does.

PSALM 145:13, NIV

$\mathcal{D}$*o you remember where the spies were hiding?* They were quietly hiding on Rahab's roof under the flax plants. The king's messengers were at the door: Boom! Boom! Boom! Rahab opened the door. The king's men said, "Bring out the men who came to your house because they're spies!"

Rahab told them, "The men did come by, but they left at dark when the city gate was closing. If you go after them quickly, you might catch up to them." So the messengers set out on the road to pursue the spies. Rahab could have said the spies were on the roof, but she didn't want the Israelite men to be harmed.

Rahab climbed to the roof and told them, "I know that God has given this land to the Israelites." *So, from Rahab's words, what was the big reason she protected the spies?*

Rahab said, "Here in Jericho, we heard that your God dried

up the water in the Red Sea to protect you from the Egyptians. I know that your God is the LORD of both heaven and earth." *What is Rahab saying she believes about God?*

Rahab then asked the spies to promise that they would protect her family when the army came to conquer Jericho. *Do you think the spies agreed?*

The spies asked for a promise in return: "If you don't tell anyone what we're doing, we will be kind to you when God gives us the land." *Why was it important for Rahab and the spies to keep their promises to each other?*

Through her window, Rahab let the men down by a rope. Rahab whispered to the spies: "Go to the hills so the soldiers won't find you. Hide for three days. Then it will be safe to leave."

The spies told Rahab to tie a scarlet cord to the window and keep her family inside during the battle. Then they'd be protected. *Why do you think the spies told her to tie the scarlet cord to the window?*

The spies then ran to the hills and hid. The king's men searched for the spies, but they didn't find them. After three days, the spies returned to Joshua and said, "The LORD has surely given us this land."

The scarlet cord hung from Rahab's window as the Israelites prepared to take over the city of Jericho. God told Joshua and his men to march around the city wall for six days. On the seventh day, God said to march around the city seven times, to blow trumpets, and to give a loud shout. They did just what God told them, and the walls of Jericho collapsed. Then the Israelites charged into the city and conquered it. *What do you think happened to Rahab and her family?*

The Israelite men kept their promise and brought Rahab and her entire family to safety. Hebrews 11 says that Rahab and her family were protected because of Rahab's faith. God remembered Rahab, and she became one of the women in Jesus' family line!

 **QUESTIONS**

- How did Rahab's actions have a part in the Israelites reaching the Promised Land?
- Why is it important to do what you say you will do?
- What is beautiful about Rahab's heart?

 PRAYER

God, thank You for the promises fulfilled in this passage. Help us to be trustworthy people who keep promises. We're thankful that Rahab chose to believe in You. We pray You would help us to always have faith and believe in You. In Jesus' name, amen.

 DAUGHTERS IN ACTION

Rahab's account is full of promises: Rahab promising not to turn in the Israelite spies, the spies promising to protect Rahab's family, and God's promise of the Promised Land.

Explain to your daughter that people who keep promises are trustworthy.

This week, if your daughter makes a promise to clean her room or play with her sibling, discuss how important it is that she keeps her promise. Explain to your daughter that the promises she makes should be good promises. Be a good example to your daughter by following through with what you say you will do.

 CREATIVE FUN

Materials: Scissors, red paper, pen, stapler

This week, keep track of how you both fulfill promises by building a paper chain "rope" together to represent the rope Rahab used. Cut fourteen strips of red paper, each one a few inches wide. Write one word from the second sentence of Psalm 145:13 on each slip of paper. Staple the strip that says *The* in a loop, and hang it from a window. Put the stapler and the other paper strips nearby. Every time one of you keeps a promise, add the next loop to your paper chain rope. See if you can keep so many promises that your rope completes the verse by the end of the week.

8

RISING UP
—DEBORAH

(Judges 4–5)

Words for Your Heart

Each of you should use whatever gift
you have received to serve others.

I PETER 4:10, NIV

When *have you forgotten something really important?* Well, for some time, the Israelites forgot about God. They also did wrong things that angered the Lord. Because of their choices, God allowed them to be defeated by Jabin, a king of Canaan. Sisera was the commander of Jabin's army. He had nine hundred iron chariots, and he treated the Israelite people cruelly for twenty years.

The Israelites finally remembered the Lord and cried out in prayer. *Do you think the Lord showed mercy and listened to the Israelites?* He did. God raised up a courageous woman named Deborah to help them.

Deborah was a leader and a judge in Israel. The Israelites came to her court to have their arguments decided. Her court was located under a palm tree called the Palm of Deborah in the hill country of Ephraim. *If you had a court under a palm tree, what would you name it?*

God gave Deborah a gift—a special ability. First Peter 4:10 tells us to use the gifts God gives us to serve others. We can use God's gifts to serve Him, just as Deborah did. The Lord gave Deborah the gift of being a prophetess like Miriam, Moses' sister. *Do you remember what a prophetess is?* It means that the Lord gave that person messages to share with others.

Deborah relayed a message from God to a military leader named Barak. She said, "The LORD commands you: 'Take ten thousand men with you to Mount Tabor. I will draw Sisera and his army to the Kishon River and give him over to you.'" *Do you think Barak went or was too afraid to go?*

Barak told Deborah, "If you go with me, I'll go. But if you don't go, then I'm not going." *How do you think Barak felt taking ten thousand soldiers to attack Sisera?* Everyone feels afraid sometimes, but when you feel this way, remember that God is with you.

Deborah answered, "I will go with you. But now the honor won't be yours. God will hand Sisera over to a woman." Deborah was a strong and confident woman. She continued telling God's message. *Where do you think Deborah got her confidence from?*

Sisera, the evil leader, heard that Barak and his soldiers were at Mount Tabor. So he gathered his nine hundred chariots and went to meet them for a battle.

Remember that Deborah was a prophetess. She told Barak, "Go! Today you will win against Sisera. God has gone ahead of you." *What do Deborah's words tell you about her confidence in God?*

After seeing Deborah's confidence in the Lord, Barak chose to have faith in Him. Barak went strongly into battle, followed by his ten thousand men. The Lord confused Sisera's men, and they panicked. The Lord defeated Sisera's army, and Sisera abandoned his chariot and ran away.

The Lord won the battle that day, and Deborah and Barak overcame the cruel Sisera! The great strength of the Lord is far more powerful than anything. Deborah and Barak didn't forget about God like the other Israelites had in the past. Instead, they trusted Him for their victory. They sang this song in celebration:

"Listen, kings. Pay attention, rulers!
I myself will sing to the LORD.
I will make music to the LORD, the God of Israel."

? QUESTIONS

- How did Deborah's confidence in the Lord encourage Barak to change?
- How can we have confidence like Deborah when we feel afraid?
- What is beautiful about Deborah's heart?

✚ PRAYER

Lord, thank You for Deborah's bravery and confidence in You. When we are afraid, please help us be leaders who are brave and confident like she was. In Jesus' name, amen.

⚑ DAUGHTERS IN ACTION

Just as Deborah was a confident leader, your daughter can practice being a leader by planning a volunteer outreach with family and friends. Help her brainstorm her God-given gifts and how she could use her gifts to help others. For example, if one of her gifts is art, she could draw or paint pictures to give to an elderly person. If it's singing, she could sing a song at a nursing home. If it's being a hard worker, she could offer to do a single parent's yard work.

If your daughter is good at organizing, she could help organize a food pantry or clothing at a shelter, or if she's gifted at cooking, she could prepare a meal for a struggling family.

Once the project is chosen, decide which friends and family members you'd like to invite to help.

 CREATIVE FUN

Materials: Supplies for making invitations

With your daughter, create invitations for the people you're asking to help you with the Daughters in Action volunteer outreach. Include the what, when, where, and why details. Deliver the invitations and have fun volunteering together.

9

WHERE YOU GO, I'LL GO —RUTH AND NAOMI

(Ruth 1)

Words for Your Heart

A friend loves at all times.

PROVERBS 17:17

A long time ago, a woman named Naomi lived in Bethlehem. She was married to Elimelech (E-lim-i-lek), and they had two sons. Their town had a famine, which means they ran out of food. *Can you imagine not being able to eat breakfast, lunch, or dinner for a long time?* They were hungry and needed to find food, so their family moved to a land called Moab.

Naomi's husband died, and her two sons married women from Moab, named Ruth and Orpah. After living in Moab for ten years, Ruth and Orpah's husbands died too, so the three women were widows. This made them very sad.

Naomi decided she would return to her hometown of Bethlehem because the Lord had provided food there again. *If you were traveling back to your hometown after a famine, what is one food you would hope was there?*

Naomi began the journey back to Bethlehem, and Ruth and Orpah started along with her. As they walked along the road, Naomi said, "Ruth and Orpah, you've been very kind to me, but you should go back. You should stay here in Moab. May God show kindness to you. Perhaps He will bring each of you another husband."

Ruth and Orpah both cried and said, "No. We will go back with you to your people."

But Naomi insisted they stay in their hometown since she had nothing to give them. Naomi did a beautiful thing by looking out for Ruth and Orpah's needs before her own. *What is a way you can put a friend or sibling ahead of yourself like Naomi did?*

They wept again, and Orpah kissed her mother-in-law goodbye and left. *What do you think Ruth did?*

Ruth clung to Naomi and said, "Where you go, I will go. Where you stay, I will stay. Your people will become my people. Your God will become my God." Ruth was willing to leave everything behind to care for Naomi and worship the one true God.

Naomi realized Ruth was determined to go with her, so the two women journeyed to Bethlehem together. *Why do you think it might have been difficult for Ruth to leave her home and live in a new town?*

Thinking of others before yourself like Ruth and Naomi did is a great way to love people. Next time you want to go first or play with something that everyone wants, try sharing or letting someone go ahead of you—you will be showing the love of Jesus.

When Naomi and Ruth arrived in Bethlehem after their long journey, the harvest had started. The harvesters were gathering barley, which is a grain used to make bread and other foods. *If you wanted to bake the best-tasting bread in the world, what ingredients would you put in it?*

Ruth and Naomi were very hungry since they had traveled for miles from Moab to Bethlehem. The only problem was that the grain wasn't theirs. *How do you think the Lord provided food for them?* We'll find out what the Bible says in the next chapter!

 ## QUESTIONS

- How did Ruth and Naomi show they cared about each other?
- When did someone let you go ahead of them or put you first? How did that make you feel?
- What is beautiful about Ruth's and Naomi's hearts?

 ## PRAYER

Lord, we are thankful that Naomi put Ruth first and that Ruth put Naomi first, not expecting anything in return. Help us care for people, not to get something from them, but out of love for them. In Jesus' name, amen.

 ## DAUGHTERS IN ACTION

It can be hard to move to a new place like Ruth did. Reach out to someone new this week. If there are families new to your neighborhood, church, or your daughter's school, take time to get to know them. One way to welcome them is to bake cookies or homemade bread to take to them.

 ## CREATIVE FUN

Materials: 1 empty plastic 8-oz. water bottle, vinegar, teaspoon, baking soda, balloon, small funnel

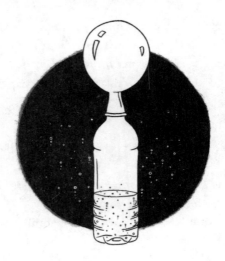

This science demonstration shows what happens when we are kind to others like Ruth was.

Explain that the balloon symbolizes a person's heart and the baking soda symbolizes kindness. Tell your daughter that you're going to explore what happens to our hearts and others' hearts when we show kindness to one another.

As we extend kindness to others and love them like Jesus calls us to do, their hearts and our hearts fill up, just like the balloon in this experiment!

1. Fill the bottle halfway with vinegar.

2. Add a teaspoon of baking soda to the balloon using the funnel. If you don't have a funnel, use the teaspoon.

3. Attach the balloon around the top of the water bottle without dropping the baking soda into the vinegar. Have your daughter make a hypothesis, or a good guess, about what will happen when the baking soda mixes with the vinegar.

4. Now lift the balloon gently so it stays attached and the baking soda drops from the balloon into the bottle. (Don't put your face close to it.)

What happens? The balloon blows up!

Ask your daughter: *What happens to our hearts and others' hearts when we show kindness to one another?*

Next time, add two teaspoons of baking soda instead of one to show what happens when you add more "kindness"!

Note: Balloons can be a choking hazard for children under seven. Be sure your daughter does not put the balloon in her mouth, and be sure to dispose of it properly after the activity.

10

A FAITHFUL
WOMAN—RUTH

(Ruth 2–4)

Words for Your Heart

The fruit of the Spirit is love, joy, peace, patience,
kindness, goodness, faithfulness, gentleness, self-control.

GALATIANS 5:22-23, ESV

*A*fter traveling from Moab to Bethlehem, Ruth and Naomi were very hungry. Since the barley harvest had begun, Ruth searched for a field where she could gather grain so that she and Naomi wouldn't go hungry.

In those days, poor people were allowed to collect grain that the workers missed when they were harvesting the field. This was called gleaning. Sometimes generous farmers left extra grain in the field on purpose so that poor people would have more grain to glean.

Soon Ruth found a field where she was allowed to glean. She worked hard throughout the day and didn't give up. *If you're cleaning up or doing chores, how can you have a good attitude and not give up like Ruth?*

Boaz, the owner of the field, noticed Ruth working. He was a relative of Naomi. Boaz saw Ruth in his field and asked a worker, "Who is that woman in the fields?"

The worker answered, "She came back from Moab with Naomi. She asked for permission to glean here, and she hasn't stopped working, except to take a short rest." *Do you think Boaz made her leave since it was his field or let her stay?*

Boaz told Ruth, "Stay in this field. And whenever you are thirsty, go and get a drink from the water jars."

Ruth asked, "Why have you been so kind to me? I'm a foreigner."

He replied, "I've been told about what you have done for Naomi, and how you left your home to come to a new place where you didn't know anyone. May the LORD richly reward you." *What quality about Ruth does Boaz seem to like?*

At mealtime, Boaz invited Ruth to eat with him and the harvesters. Ruth ate all she wanted, and there were even leftovers!

Boaz told the workers to leave extra grain for her so that she had plenty.

Ruth continued to show faithfulness. She stayed and gleaned in the field until evening, and then she carried the grain into town to Naomi.

When Ruth got home, the two women talked about all that had happened that day. Ruth kept working in Boaz's field until the barley harvest and the wheat harvest were finished.

After some time had passed, Naomi encouraged Ruth to visit Boaz again. Ruth did just as Naomi asked her to, putting on her best clothes and perfume.

Boaz was glad to see Ruth again. He said, "Everyone in town knows that you are a woman of noble character." *Did Boaz notice how she looked or the kind of woman she was?*

After they had spent some time together, Boaz said, "Don't go back to your mother-in-law empty-handed." Then he gave Ruth six portions of barley to take home to Naomi! Boaz was a thoughtful man.

What do you think eventually happened between Boaz and Ruth? They were married! Ruth later gave birth to a son named Obed, who became the grandfather of King David. *Who else do you think was part of their family line?* Jesus! How amazing that God included faithful Ruth and generous Boaz in Jesus' family line!

 ## QUESTIONS

- What miracle came many years later after Ruth stayed with Naomi?
- What quality of the fruit of the Spirit did Ruth have, and how did she show it? (These are listed in the verse at the beginning of this devotion.)
- What is beautiful about Ruth's heart?

 ## PRAYER

Lord, help us to be faithful by working hard in all we do and also to show others the fruit of Your Spirit like Ruth did. In Jesus' name, amen.

DAUGHTERS IN ACTION

Materials: Dry-erase marker

The fruit of the Spirit was evident in Ruth's life. The fruit of the Spirit includes nine qualities that come from the Holy Spirit: love, joy, peace, patience, kindness, goodness, faithfulness, gentleness, and self-control. With your daughter, choose one quality of the fruit of the Spirit to show more of this week. Use a dry-erase marker to write it on your mirrors. Each time you see it, pray something like this: *Lord, please help me show more (quality).* Every day, do one thing to practice that quality. Then, share about your experience with each other at the end of the day.

 CREATIVE FUN

Materials: Nine smooth rocks, permanent marker, jar or small container

Find nine rocks outside. On each rock, write a quality of the fruit of the Spirit with a permanent marker. Place the rocks in a jar or small container. During dinnertime this week, have each family member pick a rock and share how someone in the family has demonstrated that quality.

11

HEARD BY THE LORD—HANNAH

(1 Samuel 1)

Words for Your Heart

Cast all your anxiety on him because he cares for you.

1 PETER 5:7, NIV

*H*annah was married to a man named Elkanah, who loved her a lot. Hannah did not have any children, even though she wanted a baby very much.

There was a woman close to Hannah who did have children. For years, she teased Hannah about not having a baby. Whenever Hannah and Elkanah traveled to the house of the Lord to worship, the woman bothered Hannah so much that Hannah would cry. *What would you have said to Hannah if you were there?*

One day when Hannah was in the house of the Lord, she stood and cried to the Lord in prayer. Hannah trusted God with her sadness. She knew she could talk to Him about it. *If someone teases you or you feel sad, what can you also do?* When you have a tough day, remember that God loves you. He is always there for you, and you can talk to Him about anything that's on your mind. *Why do you think God wants to hear your prayers?*

When Hannah prayed, she made a promise to the Lord that if He granted her a son, she would dedicate him to the Lord.

Eli the priest was in the temple that day. He saw Hannah praying, and he was concerned. He didn't understand what she was doing. Hannah explained to Eli that she was pouring out her heart to the Lord, telling Him about her grief because she didn't have a baby.

Eli understood. Then he told her, "May God grant to you what you've asked."

The next morning, Hannah and her husband, Elkanah, got up and worshipped one last time before they went back to their home. Hannah knew that Eli had told her that God would answer her prayer. *What is something you have really wanted and prayed for, but have had to wait for?* It was probably difficult for Hannah to wait for what she wanted. *What do you think helped her wait?* When it seems like your prayer isn't answered right away, remember that you can trust God.

In due time, God gave Hannah a son! After Hannah had her son, she named him Samuel, which means "heard by God." *Why do you think she gave him this name?* Hannah said, "I prayed for this child, and the LORD has given him to me. So I will give him to the LORD." Hannah was faithful and dedicated Samuel to the Lord just as she had promised. The Lord was with Samuel as he grew up, and he became a prophet.

Hannah celebrated God's gift with this prayer: "My heart rejoices in the LORD. . . . There is no one besides You! And there is no rock like our God" (1 Samuel 2:1-2).

The Lord was gracious to Hannah and gave her three more sons and two daughters!

QUESTIONS

- What did Hannah do after the woman teased her?
- When Hannah was sad, how did she show her faithfulness to the Lord? What about when she was happy?
- What is beautiful about Hannah's heart?

 ## PRAYER

Lord, just as Hannah prayed whether she was happy or sad, help us do the same. Thank You, Lord, for hearing us and answering us when we share what's on our hearts. Help us to always trust You. In Jesus' name, amen.

 ## DAUGHTERS IN ACTION

Just like Hannah's children, every child in the world has a birth story! Share details of your daughter's birth story with her, such as the time she was born, how you chose her name, whether she cried or smiled a lot, and what you thought about her when you first saw her. Your daughter may also enjoy hearing the rest of the family's birth stories and making a booklet or video about them to celebrate God's gift of family.

CREATIVE FUN

Materials: Clasps, bracelet wire or string, decorative beads, letter beads

Make beaded bracelets together as a reminder to pray. To make the bracelet, knot one part of the clasp to the wire or string, and add decorative beads that remind you of people or things you'd like to pray about. Then use letter beads to spell the word PRAY. Knot the string at the other end with the connecting part of the clasp. Wear the bracelets as a reminder to pray when you're happy and when you're sad. Throughout the week, tell each other about times you noticed your bracelet and stopped to pray.

12

PURSUING PEACE
—ABIGAIL

(1 Samuel 25)

Words for Your Heart

Those who promote peace have joy.

PROVERBS 12:20

*A*bigail was a beautiful, intelligent woman who cared about the needs of others. She was married to a rich and mean man named Nabal who owned a thousand goats and three thousand sheep. *If you could have three thousand of any animal, which one would you pick?*

One day, David and his army were close to Nabal's property. David had been a shepherd, but now he was leading an army and soon he would be king of Israel.

While David and his army were in the desert, they needed food and supplies. In the past, when Nabal's shepherds were near David, David and his men protected them and treated them well. David thought it made sense to send some of his men to ask Nabal for help.

But Nabal said, "Who is this David? Why should I share my

things with these men I don't even know?" *Do you think Nabal was a happy man?* Probably not, because selfishness can make a person unhappy.

The men went back and told David that Nabal wouldn't help him. David was angry and ready to fight Nabal. He took four hundred men along with him and told them, "Strap on your swords!"

One of the servants hurried to find Abigail. As soon as he saw her, he said, "David's messengers asked Nabal for help, but Nabal shouted insults at them. David's men have been so good to us. Think about what to do because disaster is coming our way!" *What do you think Abigail did?*

Abigail lost no time. She gathered two hundred loaves of bread, roasted grain, sheep, one hundred clusters of raisins, two hundred fig cakes, and drinks to bring to David and his men. *The load was*

too heavy to carry, so how do you think she brought it to them? There weren't cars or buses back then, so she loaded the food and drinks on donkeys.

David was angry, and he said to his men, "I wasted my time protecting Nabal's property in the desert. He's paid me evil for the good I did for him."

As David was planning to get back at Nabal, Abigail arrived. She quickly approached David and said, "Please don't pay any attention to what Nabal said. I'm sorry—I should have been the one to see your men. Please give these gifts to the men who follow you."

Remember, David and his men had their swords ready to attack. But Abigail wisely asked David to reconsider his attack on Nabal. She said, "When you are a leader of Israel, you don't want to feel guilty about taking revenge on us."

David knew that Abigail was right. He replied, "Praise the LORD for sending you to me today. You have kept me from attacking Nabal. May God bless you for your good judgment. Go home in peace."

Why do you think David was glad that Abigail came right when she did? Ecclesiastes 10:4 tells us that "calmness puts great offenses to rest." Abigail's peacefulness stopped a battle between Nabal and David.

❓ QUESTIONS

- How did Abigail make peace with David?
- If your siblings or friends say something rude to you or if you're frustrated with them, how can you keep the peace and get along instead of arguing?
- What is beautiful about Abigail's heart?

PRAYER

Lord, I pray we would be quick to try and keep peace with our family and friends. And, just as Abigail helped David, please show us ways we can help people in need. In Jesus' name, amen.

DAUGHTERS IN ACTION

Materials: Supplies to cook a meal

Just as Abigail brought food to David and his men, bring a meal to a single parent, a widow, a program that helps homeless families, or some family friends. Let your daughter lead the grocery shopping to find the needed ingredients. Cook the meal together, and have fun decorating a dessert and a card with some Bible verses to go with the meal!

CREATIVE FUN

Materials: Paper, pen, a small reward

Encourage your daughter to practice peacemaking with this fun activity.

1. Create a chart with your daughter like the one in the picture. Write Proverbs 12:20 on the top.

2. At the bottom of the paper, cut five slits to create six pull-off slips of paper. Come up with six reward ideas with your daughter, such as staying up thirty minutes later, having a treat of her choice, having thirty minutes on the computer, or watching a TV show. Write one reward on each slip of paper.

3. Each time your daughter chooses to be a peacemaker, whether she responds kindly to a rude comment, forgives

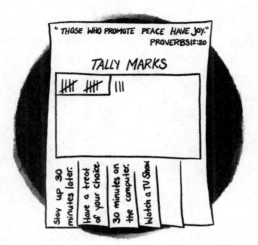

someone, asks for forgiveness, chooses not to argue, or keeps the peace in some other way, give her a tally. You may also give a tally if she memorizes the verse on the chart.

4. Once she earns a predetermined number of tallies, such as five tallies if she's younger or ten if she's older, have her rip a reward off the bottom of the paper to redeem. Then start over with the tallies so she can earn another reward.

13

SEEKING WISDOM
—THE QUEEN OF SHEBA

(1 Kings 3, 10)

Words for Your Heart

If any of you lacks wisdom, he should ask God,
who gives to all generously.

JAMES 1:5

$\mathcal{S}$olomon, the third king of Israel, was known everywhere for his great wisdom. He wrote the book of Ecclesiastes in the Bible and much of the book of Proverbs. *How do you think Solomon got to be so wise?*

One night the Lord appeared to Solomon and said to him, "Ask for whatever you'd like Me to give you." *What do you think Solomon asked for?* He asked God to give him wisdom and knowledge so that he could rule his kingdom and its people well. That's all Solomon asked for.

God was pleased with Solomon's request. He said, "Since you asked for wisdom, I will give it to you. Your wisdom will be greater than anyone's. I will also give you what you did not ask for. You will have riches and honor. During your lifetime no other king will be as great as you." *Why do you think God was so pleased with what Solomon asked for?*

Word of Solomon's great wisdom spread throughout the land. The queen of Sheba heard about Solomon's fame and his relationship with God. She wanted to know more about Solomon, so she traveled a long way to Jerusalem to see him—about 1,200 miles! One mile is four laps around a typical running track, so her trip to see him would have been almost five thousand laps around a track!

The queen of Sheba journeyed through desert lands to see Solomon. She traveled with a great caravan of camels carrying gifts of spices, gold, and precious stones. *If you could have traveled on an animal to visit Solomon, which animal would you have chosen?*

The queen of Sheba wanted to talk to Solomon about everything on her mind. She had a lot of questions to ask him. Asking questions is a great way to learn. It's also a great way to get to know people better and to show you care about them.

When the queen saw Solomon's palace and all the wonders of his kingdom, she was amazed. The queen tested Solomon with hard questions, but none of them were too difficult for him to answer. The queen was very impressed with his great wisdom.

Proverbs 2:4-6 says, "If you seek [wisdom] like silver and search for it like hidden treasure, then you will understand the fear of the LORD and discover the knowledge of God. For the LORD gives wisdom." *So, how can we get wisdom?*

Once the queen of Sheba had spent time with Solomon, she said, "The report I heard in my country about your wisdom is true. Praise be to God, who has delighted in you and made you king of Israel because of His eternal love for Israel. You have become king so that justice and righteousness will be a part of this kingdom."

Then she offered him the gifts of spices, gold, and precious stones that she had brought from her own country. *If you had visited Solomon, what gift would you have brought him?*

 QUESTIONS

- How did the queen of Sheba discover for herself that Solomon was truly wise?
- In what area of your life do you need wisdom or help from God?
- What is beautiful about the queen of Sheba's heart?

 PRAYER

Lord, just as the queen of Sheba searched for wisdom, we also pray for wisdom. Please guide us in our decisions and following You. In Jesus' name, amen.

 DAUGHTERS IN ACTION

Materials: A small treasure to hide

Hide a treasure such as a dollar bill, coins, or chocolate candies in a room for your daughter to find. Afterward, talk about ways to seek God's wisdom like it's a hidden treasure.

 CREATIVE FUN

Materials: 14 small slips of paper, pen or pencil, 7 balloons, tape

To gain wisdom, the queen of Sheba asked Solomon questions. Use this fun activity to discuss Solomon's wisdom with your daughter. Find seven verses from the book of Proverbs that you'd like to talk about. Write the references to the verses on seven of the slips of paper, such as Proverbs 11:16; 13:20; 14:29; 14:30; 17:14; 18:13; and 27:2. Also write down seven questions—one on each of the remaining slips of paper—for your daughter to ask to learn more about you. Some examples are: *What did you enjoy doing when you were a kid? What was your favorite meal as a kid? What did you want to be when you grew up?*

Then roll each slip of paper. Squeeze one proverb slip and one question slip into each of the seven balloons. Blow up the balloons and tie them off. Tape the balloons to a wall in your home. Each day, pop a balloon. Together, look up the proverb and talk about it. Then have your daughter ask you the question.

Note: Balloons are a choking hazard to children under age seven. Please use caution.

14

A LITTLE OIL AND A LOT OF FAITH—THE MOTHER OF TWO SONS

(2 Kings 4)

Words for Your Heart

My God will supply all your needs according to
His riches in glory in Christ Jesus.

PHILIPPIANS 4:19

*L*ong ago there was a woman with two sons. Her husband was a prophet who followed God faithfully during his life.

But one day the woman's husband died, and she became a widow. While the man was alive, he had borrowed lots of money. After he died, the people he owed money to wanted to be paid back, but the widow didn't have enough money to repay them. She was afraid of what those people might do. *How do you think God helped her?*

The woman shared her worries with Elisha, who was a prophet of God. A prophet speaks God's truth to others just like a prophetess. Elisha didn't say, "Let me know if you need any help." Instead, he asked great questions like "How can I help you?" and "What do you have at your house?" to find out how he could help her.

The mother replied, "I have nothing except a little oil." *Do you think God could still do something with the little she had?* Yes! God is powerful, and all things are possible with Him.

Elisha said, "Ask your neighbors to bring you all their empty jars."

The woman was probably confused about why Elisha told her to get her neighbors' empty jars. But she had faith and did exactly what the prophet Elisha told her to do.

The neighbors showed the woman compassion and gave her all their empty jars. *When has a neighbor helped your family, or when have you helped a neighbor's family?* When we love one another, like Elisha and the neighbors loved the woman, we are following God's two most important commandments: to love God and love others.

Elisha told the mother to go inside her home with the empty jars and with her two boys, and then to shut the door. A miracle

was about to happen! *Why do you think Elisha wanted the woman's sons to be there also?* He then told her to fill the jars with oil.

Showing great faith, the mother started to fill the empty jars with her little bit of oil, just as the prophet Elisha told her to. As the mother poured oil into the jars, more and more oil appeared! When the mother had filled all the jars she had, she turned to her son and asked him for another jar. But the son said, "We don't have any more jars. They're all gone." And right then, the oil stopped flowing.

How do you think the full jars of oil helped the mother? Elisha said, "Go and sell the oil. Use some of the money to pay all of the money you owe. Then you and your sons can live on the money that's left over." God provided just what the mother needed through Elisha, the woman's neighbors, and her faith.

 ## QUESTIONS

- How did the mother show faith?
- God used the neighbors and Elisha to meet the mother's need. Do you know someone with a need you can meet?
- What is beautiful about the mother's heart?

 ## PRAYER

Lord, help us to have faith like the mother in this Bible passage, to help others when we can, and to ask for help when we need it. Just as You met the mother's needs, thank You for meeting our needs. In Jesus' name, amen.

 ## DAUGHTERS IN ACTION

Materials: Sidewalk chalk

In this Bible passage, Elisha and the neighbors encouraged the mother of two sons and loved her well. Show love to your neighbors by leaving fun and encouraging chalk messages on their driveway, on the sidewalk in front of their home, or on their doorstep. Make sure the area is uncovered so that the rain will eventually wash away the message. Do this when they're not home so it will be a surprise!

 CREATIVE FUN

Materials: Bowl, 1 cup flour, 2 teaspoons cream of tartar, $^1/_3$ cup salt, 1 cup water, 1 tablespoon vegetable oil, whisk, washable paint, food coloring, nonstick saucepan, spatula, waxed paper

In this activity, your daughter will make a play dough jar as a reminder to have faith that God will meet your needs.

Follow these instructions to make play dough:

1. In a bowl, combine the flour, cream of tartar, and salt.

2. Add the water and oil. Mix well with a whisk until there are no lumps.

3. If you want the dough to be different colors, put portions of the mixture into separate bowls and then add a tablespoon of washable paint or a few drops of food coloring to each bowl. Stir the play dough and enjoy watching the colors mix.

4. Pour one of the mixtures into the saucepan and put it on the stove. Mom should turn the heat to medium/low. Stir the mixture often. It will take a minute or two to start coming together. When the mixture no longer sticks to the pan as it cooks, it is ready.

5. The dough will be very hot, so use the spatula to place the dough on the plate. Let the dough cool.

6. If you made different colors of dough, repeat the steps for cooking each batch.

7. When the dough is completely cool, set out a piece of wax paper and form a jar to represent the jar from the Bible passage. Let the jar air-dry for several days. Then have your daughter paint the jar. You may want her to write Philippians 4:19 on the jar. Set the jar in a location where it will remind you both to have faith in God's provision.

Any leftover play dough can be stored in sealed plastic bags for several months.

15

SEEKING GOD FIRST —HULDAH

(2 Kings 22–23)

Words for Your Heart

Seek first the kingdom of God and His righteousness.

MATTHEW 6:33

*O*ver six hundred years before Jesus was born, Josiah became king of Judah. *How old do you think he was when he became king?* Josiah was only eight years old! *If you became queen today, what is the first thing you would do?*

During King Josiah's eighteenth year ruling the land, he had carpenters, builders, and masons repair the Temple, which was like a church. While the workers repaired the Temple, the book of the law was found, which was a book about how to follow God.

King Josiah ordered the book to be read. When the king heard the laws, he realized that for a long time, the people in his land had not followed God's laws. King Josiah was filled with sadness because of the people's sin. King Josiah wanted to learn more about God and about what was written in the book of the law.

Some of the leaders went to speak with a wise woman named Huldah. She was married to Shallum, who was in charge of the king's wardrobe. Huldah was a prophetess. *Do you remember the names of some of the prophetesses we've learned about?* Deborah and Miriam were also prophetesses. God gave them messages to share with others. Huldah put God first by listening to Him and telling His messages to the people. She cared more about pleasing God than telling people what they wanted to hear to make them happy. God wants us to care more about pleasing Him than anything else.

God told Huldah exactly what to say to the leaders. She said: "God is going to bring destruction to this place because the people have been worshipping idols instead of God." Idols are things we care more about than God. In the Ten Commandments, the Lord says we should not have any gods other than Him. And Jesus tells us to seek God's Kingdom first. *What is one way we can seek God first, before anything else, like Huldah did?*

While the Lord was angered by those who worshipped idols, He was pleased with Josiah. God gave Huldah a message for Josiah. Huldah said, "This is what the LORD says, 'When you heard what I said, you had a humble, open heart and listened. You were so sad the people had followed idols that you wept. Because of all this, I have heard you,' declares the LORD."

Because Josiah was sorry for the people's sin, the Lord did not bring disaster to Judah during his life. Josiah ordered all the idols to be burned and the statues to be smashed to pieces. *Why do you think he did this?* The Bible says that there was never a king before or after Josiah who turned to the Lord like he did, with all his mind, heart, and strength.

The Lord, Josiah, and the people trusted Huldah because she relayed God's message honestly. *How can you also be a person people trust?* Years later, Jesus shared with His followers that those who can be trusted with little can also be trusted with much (Luke 16:10). If you are honest in the small things, people will know they can trust you with bigger things.

? QUESTIONS
- Why do you think God chose Huldah to share His message with Josiah and the other leaders?
- How did Huldah put God first and show she cared more about pleasing Him than anyone else?
- What is beautiful about Huldah's heart?

✝ PRAYER
Father, help us to be trustworthy like Huldah was. Help us to always put You first and care more about what You think than what other people think just as Huldah did. Please forgive us for times we haven't done that. Thank You, Lord. In Jesus' name, amen.

DAUGHTERS IN ACTION
Seek God first this week. One way to do that is to pray and read a Bible verse in the morning after you wake up. Then, at breakfast, talk about what you learned during your time of seeking God first.

CREATIVE FUN
Materials: Spaghetti noodles, mini marshmallows

Build models of a church using uncooked spaghetti noodles and mini marshmallows. The marshmallows hold the spaghetti together and serve as connecting pieces for your creation. You may want to use a piece of Styrofoam as a base. Alternatively, you can

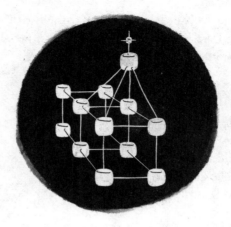

build your church with paper towel tubes and other materials. Display a tiny "book of the law" inside the church with Matthew 6:33 written on it.

16

WHO WILL BECOME QUEEN?—ESTHER

(Esther 1–2)

Words for Your Heart

*Children, obey your parents in everything,
for this pleases the Lord.*

COLOSSIANS 3:20

*L*ong ago, there was a king who ruled over many lands. He lived in a grand palace in Susa with gardens that had white and violet curtains and marble pillars. There were even gold and silver couches! *If you had a castle, what would you want it to look like?*

One day Queen Vashti refused to listen to the king, and he was very angry. The king's men said he should search for a new queen to replace her, and the king agreed.

Esther was one of the many young women brought to the castle. She was an orphan—this means she didn't have a mom or dad. Esther's cousin Mordecai adopted her and became her father. In the book of James, we learn that God is pleased when His followers take care of orphans and widows. *Why do you think caring for orphans and widows is important to the Lord?*

Before Esther was brought to the palace, Mordecai warned her not to tell the king that she was a Jew. Mordecai was afraid the king might send her away if he knew. Esther was careful to do as Mordecai said. She knew that God had given her Mordecai as a parent and that Mordecai wanted good things for her, so she trusted and obeyed him. We honor God when we respect and listen to our parents out of love for them and God. *Why do you think obeying your parents pleases God?*

Hegai, one of the king's guards, looked after Esther and the other women who were brought to the palace. He was pleased with Esther and immediately gave her beauty treatments and special food. All the young women received a year of beauty treatments before they saw the king—that's a long time! *What do you think some of the beauty treatments were?*

Every day, Mordecai paced back and forth in front of the king's gate to check on Esther and see how she was doing. Things were going well for Esther and everyone in the palace approved of her.

Hegai gave Esther advice about what to do when she saw the king, and Esther listened carefully. More than any of the other women, the king was pleased with Esther. He placed a royal crown on her head, and that day she became Queen Esther. They celebrated with mounds of delicious food and called it Esther's banquet. *If you were at Esther's banquet, what food would you hope to eat?*

After the celebration, Mordecai was sitting at the king's gate. Two of the king's officers who guarded the doorway secretly planned to kill the king. Mordecai found out about the plan. He told Esther about the men's evil plot. As soon as Esther heard, she told the king, and the two men were punished. The king was saved because of Esther and Mordecai, and it was written down in the king's book so it would always be remembered.

QUESTIONS

- Why do you think Esther followed Mordecai's advice?
- How does doing what your parents say show them you love them?
- What is beautiful about Esther's heart?

 PRAYER

Lord, we are thankful that Mordecai took care of Esther. We pray for orphans and widows—please provide for them, be with them, and show us how we can help. Just as Esther listened to and obeyed Mordecai, help us also to listen well and be respectful. In Jesus' name, amen.

 DAUGHTERS IN ACTION

Caring for orphans is close to the heart of God. If you're able to, support a family who is adopting a child or sponsor a child with an organization that supports children in need.

 CREATIVE FUN

Materials: Small jar, marbles, a reward

Use a small jar this week to help your daughter listen well, like Esther did. Decorate the outside of the jar with paint or permanent markers. Another idea is to tape construction paper around the jar and use markers and stickers to decorate it. Every time you ask your daughter to do something and she obeys the first time you ask, have her drop a marble into the jar. When the marble jar is full, celebrate with a reward, such as going out for ice cream, letting her pick out a book to purchase, having a mother-daughter movie night, or enjoying beauty treatments together. While Esther's beauty treatments included oils and perfumes, you might have more fun just painting each other's nails!

17

A TOUGH CHOICE —ESTHER

(Esther 3–6)

Words for Your Heart

Love the Lord your God with all your heart, with all your soul, and with all your mind. This is the greatest and most important command. The second is like it: Love your neighbor as yourself.

MATTHEW 22:37-39

*E*sther had become queen, and everything was fine—that is, until Haman came along. Haman was the leader of the king's army, and he was mean. He had the king's signet ring. This meant Haman had power to create laws that everyone had to follow. *If you could create one law or rule for everyone to follow, what would it be?*

Haman used the ring for evil. He sent out an order to kill all Jews. Remember that Esther was Jewish, but the king didn't know that. When Mordecai and the Jewish people heard of Haman's plan to harm them, they wept. Mordecai told the guard, "Please tell Esther to beg the king to save our people."

Esther received Mordecai's message, but she was scared to go to the king. If anyone approached him without being invited, that person could be in a lot of trouble. The only way for the person to be safe was if the king extended his golden rod. *While Esther had always listened to Mordecai, how do you think she felt about doing what he asked now?*

Mordecai sent this message to her: "Maybe you have become queen for such a time as this." Esther had to choose: Would she put loving God and others first by trying to save the Jewish people or only look out for herself? *What do you think she did?*

Esther bravely decided to see the king. *Do you remember what God's greatest two commandments are?* Just what Esther did: to love God and love others. Esther sent a reply to Mordecai: "Gather all the Jews who are in Susa and pray for me for three days and nights." *Before rushing to see the king, what did Esther first want to happen?*

After three days, Esther went to see the king. When the king saw Queen Esther, he extended his golden rod. He was pleased she came to see him! The king asked, "Queen Esther, what is your request?" Esther asked the king and Haman to come to several banquets with her.

Haman went home and bragged to all his friends that the queen invited him to dinner. But his hatred for Mordecai grew each day.

That night, the king couldn't sleep, so he ordered someone to read from the book that recorded everything that had happened while he was king. *Do you remember what was written about Mordecai in the book?* Mordecai had saved the king's life from the two men who were planning to kill him.

When the king remembered what Mordecai had done, he was so grateful that he let Mordecai ride on his royal horse. Guess who had to lead Mordecai around town chanting, "This is what's done for the man the king delights in!"? Haman! *How do you think Haman felt about that?*

At the banquet, the king asked Esther, "What is your request?"

Esther said, "Save my people, the Jewish people. Someone has planned to destroy us!"

The king yelled, "Who would dare to do this?"

Queen Esther replied, "Our enemy is Haman."

Haman was terrified. The king took the signet ring away from Haman and gave it to Mordecai, and the king ordered Haman to be punished. Haman lost everything because of jealousy and his selfish and cruel choices.

Esther fell at the king's feet weeping and begging him to end Haman's evil plan. The king told Esther and Mordecai to write a new law that would save the Jews. So Mordecai wrote a new law and sent messengers on the king's fastest horses to all the king's lands to save the Jewish people.

Celebrations filled the lands. Esther's bravery, motivated by her love for God and others, led to the Jewish people being saved!

? QUESTIONS

- How did Esther love God and others?
- What can help you be brave and do the right thing when you're afraid or people around you are doing the wrong thing?
- What is beautiful about Esther's heart?

✢ PRAYER

Lord, help us to love You and others right where You've placed us, just as Esther did. When we have to make tough decisions, please give us wisdom and courage to do the right thing. In Jesus' name, amen.

⮂ DAUGHTERS IN ACTION

Esther realized God made her queen in order to make a difference. Explain to your daughter that she can make a difference right where God has placed her. A way to do this is by praying for someone in your community, just as Esther's community prayed for her. You can also pray for people around the world who are being persecuted because they believe in Jesus.

CREATIVE FUN

Materials: Cardstock; tape; scissors; glue; various decorations such as sequins, stickers, pom-poms, and beads

Help your daughter make a crown like Queen Esther's. Cut out two wide rectangular bands from cardstock and tape them together to form a strip. Wrap it around your daughter's head so it fits well, then tape it closed. Cut triangles along the top of the band so the crown has points. Then glue pom-poms to the points. Decorate the crown with sequins, stickers, beads, and more pom-poms.

18

MORE VALUABLE
THAN RUBIES—THE WIFE
OF NOBLE CHARACTER

(Proverbs 31)

Words for Your Heart

Whatever you do, do it enthusiastically,

as something done for the Lord.

COLOSSIANS 3:23

*H*i! My name's Gabby. *What's your name?* Sometimes my mom calls me Curious Gabby because I love reading and exploring. *What do you like to do?* I'm in the attic right now looking through old boxes to see what cool things I can find.

There's something at the bottom of this box that's pretty dusty. It looks like an old Bible. Oh, cool! My great-grandma's name is written inside it. This must've been her Bible! Let's flip through it.

Proverbs 31 is underlined a whole lot so it must have been pretty special to her. Part of the chapter is called "The Wife of Noble Character." The first verse in this section says, "A wife of noble character . . . is worth far more than rubies" (v. 10, NIV). I know rubies are worth a whole lot, so noble character must be pretty important. My teacher told us that great character is when someone has integrity by being honest and working hard. That pretty much describes my dad. *Who do you know like that?*

The next part says that this woman's husband "has full confidence in her" (v. 11) and that "she brings him good" (v. 12). The wife of noble character "selects wool and flax and works with eager hands" (v. 13). *Do you have any chores or ways you help out at your house?* My chore yesterday was pulling weeds, and I wanted to give up after one minute. But my mom told me we love and honor the Lord when we work hard, so we played music and did the chore together. We actually ended up having fun! *Do you have any ideas to make helping out more fun?*

The wife of noble character "gets up while it is still night; she provides food for her family" (v. 15). Sometimes I forget how much my mom does for me. The next time she wakes up early to make breakfast, I'm going to make sure I thank her and help clean up! My favorite breakfast is my mom's chocolate chip pancakes with strawberries on top! *What's yours?*

This woman "considers a field and buys it; out of her earnings she plants a vineyard" (v. 16). This woman sure must be smart to do all that! If I could plant anything, I'd probably plant basil because I love basil pesto—yum! *If you could plant anything, what would you plant?*

"Gabby! Dinner's ready!"

Sorry, I need to go—my mom's calling me for dinner. I hope we're eating my mom's famous chocolate chip pancakes tonight! *What do you think you're having for dinner?* My mom sometimes jokes about cooking frog legs, but I sure hope that's not for dinner—yuck! The next time we get together, we'll have to tell each other what we had!

I'd love to meet again soon to read more about the wife of noble character. I'll put the Bible in a secret spot by the stairs so we can find it. I can't wait to see what happens next!

 **QUESTIONS**
- In what ways did the wife of noble character love her family well?
- Why does God want us to have a good attitude while doing chores or cleaning up?
- What is beautiful about the wife of noble character's heart?

 PRAYER

Lord, I pray that we would have noble character like this woman. Help us to love those around us well by working hard with joyful hearts. In Jesus' name, amen.

 DAUGHTERS IN ACTION

Materials: Dry-erase marker

Encourage your daughter to do her chores with a joyful heart. If she doesn't have a chore, ask her to help out in some way. Write Colossians 3:23 on your mirrors with a dry-erase marker to help you work hard for the Lord.

 CREATIVE FUN

Materials: Seeds, pot, soil

Just as the wife of noble character planted a vineyard, plant something together. Take care to water it and watch it grow over time. Explain to your daughter that just as seeds grow into plants when they get water and sunlight, our faith grows when we read the Bible, love others, and pray.

19

A GIVING HEART—THE WIFE OF NOBLE CHARACTER

(Proverbs 31)

Words for Your Heart

One who is kind to the needy honors Him.

PROVERBS 14:31

*H*ey! It's Gabby, and I'm exploring the attic again. I'm so glad you met me here! *So do you want to know what I had for dinner last week?* Not frog legs, thankfully. We had chocolate chip pancakes with strawberries—hooray! They were scrumptious! *What was your favorite meal this week?* Yum! I hope the Bible is still where we left it. Let's look. . . . Yes! It's still in our secret spot. I'm excited to check out more verses together.

The wife of noble character "opens her arms to the poor and extends her hands to the needy" (Proverbs 31:20, NIV). I was frustrated the other day when I didn't get my way—I had to share my favorite toy with my brother, and I sure didn't want to. But on Saturday, we visited a shelter for homeless families, and some of the kids didn't have any toys at all. Seeing that made it a whole lot easier to share.

My mom has this saying: "More, more, more won't make you happy, but Jesus, family, and friends do." She also tells me that Jesus says it is better to give than to receive. It sure does feel good to give something away to make someone else happy. And the more I do it, the easier it gets. Let's think of something we can give away this week. *Any ideas?*

"When it snows, [the wife of noble character] has no fear for her household; for all of them are clothed in scarlet" (v. 21). I guess that means they have warm clothes. You know, my mom is really good at always making sure I have what I need too. *How does your mom make sure you're taken care of?*

How fun that the wife of noble character and her family live in a place where it snows. I love the snow! *Have you ever been snow sledding?* Gliding down the hill, just like coasting on my bike, is so fun! After playing in the snow, I love drinking hot cocoa with marshmallows! Yum! *What do you like to do outside?*

Proverbs 31 also says the wife of noble character "makes coverings for her bed" (v. 22). *Have you tried sewing anything before?* My mom and I had so much fun cutting up one of my old dresses and sewing an outfit for my doll.

The wife of noble character also makes clothes to sell! It says, "She makes linen garments and sells them, and supplies the merchants with sashes" (v. 24). That is so cool! If I could have my own business, I think I'd sell books, or maybe my mom's chocolate chip pancakes! *If you could have your own business, what would you sell?*

"Gabby! Time to set the table!"

Oh! My mom needs me now. I know my parents worked hard getting dinner ready, but I don't feel like setting the table. *What do you think I should do?* I know I should help—I bet that's what the wife of noble character would do. Hold on a minute. "Sure, Mom! Be right down."

Well, I have to go, but I hope you have a great week. I wonder if I'm having chocolate chip pancakes again. Maybe you'll have them this week! *Want to meet again soon?* I love our time together. Talk to you later!

 **QUESTIONS**
- Why did Gabby choose to stop what she was doing to set the table?
- Why is it important to give and share as the wife of noble character did?
- What is beautiful about the wife of noble character's heart?

 PRAYER
Lord, help us care more about giving to others than getting for ourselves. When we're about to make selfish choices, remind us of Your words to love God and love others. In Jesus' name, amen.

 **DAUGHTERS IN ACTION**
Help your daughter create something to give away, just as the wife of noble character gave items she made to others. Some ideas are a bookmark, a card, a hand-knitted scarf or blanket, or a bracelet.

 **CREATIVE FUN**
Just as the wife of noble character sold clothing, encourage your daughter to earn money this week by doing chores or selling something such as lemonade, cookies, books, or toys. If she sells items, help her decorate a poster listing the items and prices. Next week, she'll find out what to do with the money she earned!

20

STRENGTH AND DIGNITY—THE WIFE OF NOBLE CHARACTER

(Proverbs 31)

Words for Your Heart

Do not let any unwholesome talk come out of your mouths,
but only what is helpful for building others up according
to their needs, that it may benefit those who listen.

EPHESIANS 4:29, NIV

*H*ey! It's Gabby again! *So what did you end up having for din-*
ner after the last time we met? Well, I had a dinner I don't like—
fish sticks. But I guess that's what makes pancake dinners extra
delicious!

Hopefully the Bible's still in our secret spot. Let's go see.

Yes! Here it is. Let's read the rest of Proverbs 31. It says the wife
of noble character "is clothed with strength and dignity" (v. 25,
NIV). That's awesome. At school yesterday, a kid said something
really mean to me. I was pretty upset about it. But if it happens
again, I'm going to walk away because I know I'm clothed with
strength and dignity. I can be strong because I'm confident that
God loves me.

My mom tells me that God finds joy in me because He created

me. He feels the same way about you. I even picture God smiling at me sometimes. *What do you think God does when He thinks of you?*

The next verse says that the wife of noble character "speaks with wisdom" (v. 26). I get mad sometimes when my brother's annoying, but I'm working on being nicer to him. One time I told my mom that Jesus probably only forgives me halfway when I'm rude—I was feeling pretty guilty. She said, "No way. Jesus fully forgives you. We all mess up, but what matters is turning away from our sins, asking for forgiveness, and trying to love God and others the best we can." It's amazing that Jesus fully forgives us—*why do you think He does that?* I think it's because God loves us so much that nothing can get in the way of His love for us.

My mom and I are memorizing Ephesians 4:29 to help us speak kindly and love each other better—*want to memorize it with us?* It says, "Do not let any unwholesome talk come out of your mouths, but only what is helpful for building others up according to their needs, that it may benefit those who listen."

My goal this week is to only say nice things to my brother. *Is it hard for you to speak kindly sometimes too?* I'm so glad Jesus forgives us when we mess up and helps us to be more kind.

The next verse in Proverbs says that the woman of noble character "watches over the affairs of her household and does not eat the bread of idleness" (v. 27). She's not lazy but works hard. It also says that "beauty is fleeting; but a woman who fears the LORD is to be praised" (v. 30).

I'm seeing that outward beauty and popularity aren't important to God. *Do you think God cares more about how we look and dress or about whether we have a beautiful heart?* My dad tells me that loving God and others is what makes someone beautiful. He's even asked me this question since I was three years old: *"What makes you beautiful?"* And, years later, I always say: "My heart, mind, and soul."

So this is what it means to be a woman with noble character. Whether I get married or not, this is the kind of person I want to be. I had so much fun reading Proverbs 31 with you! Hope you have a super-duper week and that we both get to eat chocolate chip pancakes soon!

? QUESTIONS
- What makes your heart beautiful?
- Other than your mom, who in your life has qualities like the wife of noble character?
- What is beautiful about the wife of noble character's heart?

✝ PRAYER
Lord, help us speak kindly to others. If someone hurts our feelings, remind us that we are clothed with strength and confidence in You, just like the wife of noble character. Help us to care most about inner beauty and how we love You and others. In Jesus' name, amen.

▷ DAUGHTERS IN ACTION
Materials: Photo of your daughter, cardstock, glue or Mod Podge, pen

Together, look for a photo of your daughter that you can adhere to a piece of cardstock using Mod Podge or glue. Another idea is to have your daughter paint a picture of herself. Above the picture, write, "I am clothed with strength and dignity in the Lord." Find a place to hang it in her room so she is reminded of this awesome truth.

CREATIVE FUN

Your daughter could do several things with the money she earned last week. She could give it to your church or a charity. Another option is to separate the money into three categories: *Give, Save, Spend.* As your daughter continues to earn money, she could split it between the three categories. Divide the money into three envelopes, bags, or jars. If you'd like to be more creative, purchase a box with three compartments. Encourage your daughter to decorate the box and label the three categories.

21

REJOICING TOGETHER
—ELIZABETH AND MARY

(Luke 1)

Words for Your Heart

Rejoice with those who rejoice.

ROMANS 12:15

Elizabeth and her husband, Zechariah, followed the Lord's ways. They were old and didn't have any children. This made them very sad. *When have you felt sad about something you couldn't have?*

Zechariah was a priest. One day it was his turn to serve in the Temple. While he was there, an angel named Gabriel visited him. *How would you feel if an angel suddenly appeared to you?* Zechariah was surprised and afraid.

But Gabriel said to him, "Don't be afraid. God has heard your prayer. Your wife, Elizabeth, will soon have a son, and you are to name him John. He will bring you much delight. Many people will rejoice because of him. He will be great in the Lord's eyes." *Do you think Elizabeth became pregnant like the angel said she would?* She sure did!

Elizabeth gave credit to God, saying, "God has done this for me."

Elizabeth had a cousin whose name was Mary. She was engaged to a righteous man named Joseph, and they would soon be married. The angel Gabriel appeared to Mary six months after he appeared to Elizabeth's husband. He said, "Greetings! The Lord has blessed you! The Lord is with you."

Mary was scared when she saw the angel. But Gabriel said, "Don't be afraid, Mary. God is pleased with you. You will soon give birth to a son who is to be named Jesus." (*Jesus* means "savior.")

"Even though she is older, your relative Elizabeth will have a baby too. Nothing is impossible with God."

Over six hundred years before Jesus came into the world, the prophet Isaiah told people that the Savior would come to the world. Now Isaiah's words were coming true because Mary would soon give birth to Jesus!

Mary knew it was an honor to be chosen to have God's Son. She said, "I am God's servant. May it happen just as you've said." *How did Mary honor the Lord and put Him first by what she said?*

Mary hurried to Elizabeth's home to share the exciting news! When Elizabeth heard Mary's greeting, the baby inside her leaped and Elizabeth was filled with the Holy Spirit. *Do you know what the Holy Spirit does?* The Holy Spirit teaches us, guides us, strengthens us, and helps us know God.

Elizabeth said, "You are blessed, and your child will be blessed too."

Mary said to Elizabeth, "God has done great things for me— His name is holy."

Both women would soon be mothers. Mary and Elizabeth rejoiced and celebrated together.

Mary stayed with Elizabeth for about three months. They had much to celebrate—Elizabeth thought she was too old to have a baby, but God answered her prayers, and she was about to have a baby boy. Mary was a young woman, but God had chosen her to give birth to His Son, the Messiah, the Savior of the world.

Soon Elizabeth gave birth to a son, and her neighbors and relatives shared in her joy. People thought he should be named Zechariah like his father. *Do you think Elizabeth named their son Zechariah like the people said or listened to the angel?* Elizabeth confidently spoke up and said, "No! He is to be called John," just as the angel had said. Elizabeth and Zechariah's son became known as John the Baptist. And the Lord was with him.

 QUESTIONS

- What is beautiful about Mary and Elizabeth's relationship?
- When your friend or sibling does something well, how can you celebrate that person and what the Lord is doing in him or her?
- What is beautiful about Mary's and Elizabeth's hearts?

 PRAYER

Lord, we're thankful that Elizabeth and Mary rejoiced together and for Your great miracles. Help us rejoice with others and help us celebrate what You're doing in their lives, just as Mary and Elizabeth did. In Jesus' name, amen.

 DAUGHTERS IN ACTION

Materials: Cardstock, markers

Celebrate a friend or someone in your family. You and your daughter may want to make a colorful poster or create an acrostic poem. To make an acrostic poem, write the person's name vertically on a piece of cardstock. Then write a word that describes the person for each letter in her name. For example, for Beth, I could write:

Beautiful hearted
Easygoing
Thoughtful
Happy

 CREATIVE FUN

Materials: Red and green construction paper, scissors, photocopy of appendix A (pg. 182), pen, tape

Make a Christmas countdown paper chain to celebrate Jesus' birth. You can use the chain now, store it until later, or, if it's fewer than twelve days to Christmas, pull off several links each day.

1. Cut twelve strips from construction paper—six green strips and six red strips.

2. Write each of the segments from appendix A on a different paper strip. Or photocopy appendix A and cut the segments into strips. Then glue each sentence onto a different construction paper strip.

3. Write the number of the day on the back of each strip to keep the strips in order.

4. Make a loop with the day one strip and tape it closed so the writing is inside the loop. Weave the day two strip through the day one link, and tape it closed. Repeat until the paper chain is complete.

5. Hang the chain on the wall, with the day one link at the top so it will be the last link you remove.

6. Every day, have your daughter remove a link and tape it to the wall under the previous one. Together, read the story from the beginning and answer the newest question on the chain. After twelve days, you'll have the entire account of Jesus' birth on the wall!

22

THE SAVIOR
IS BORN—MARY

(Luke 2)

Words for Your Heart

Humble yourselves before the Lord, and He will exalt you.

JAMES 4:10

*J*t was almost time for Mary to have her baby. Mary and Joseph lived in a small town called Nazareth. Their village was made up of poor farmers, so it's likely that Mary and Joseph were poor too. *Why do you think God chose someone like Mary to bring His Son into the world, instead of someone like a princess or a queen?*

At that time, the ruler, Caesar Augustus, decided that it was important to count all the people who lived in the entire Roman Empire. So Mary and Joseph had to travel about eighty miles to Bethlehem to be counted in the census. These days, traveling eighty miles only takes a short time by car or bus, but back then the trip would have taken days. And because Mary was pregnant, it would have been difficult and tiring to travel.

Bringing the Son of God into the world was a huge responsibility. But because of Mary's humility and desire to serve God, she was willing to do what God had asked of her. *How do you think God felt about that?* Humility is a beautiful quality to God. When someone is humble, she doesn't just think about herself; she thinks of others, too. Mary was a selfless, humble woman who was quick to think of others.

Once Mary and Joseph arrived in Bethlehem, they searched for a place to rest so Mary could have her baby. *Do you think Jesus was born in a huge, magnificent castle?* The inns didn't have enough room for them, so they stayed in a stable where the animals lived.

It was time for Mary to have her baby. Jesus Christ, our Savior, was born that day. Today we celebrate Jesus' birth on Christmas Day. *What special word do you notice in the word* CHRISTmas?

Mary lovingly wrapped the baby in strips of cloth and placed Him in the manger. A manger is a long, open box that animals eat from. *Since God could have brought Jesus into the world in a beautiful place, why do you think He chose a simple stable?* This is a great reminder that the Lord doesn't care about riches—he cares about the heart.

Nearby shepherds were taking care of their sheep. It was important to watch over the sheep at nighttime to protect them. Suddenly an angel appeared, and God's glory shone all around the shepherds.

The shepherds were very scared, but the angel said, "Don't be afraid. I have good, joyful news for you. Today the Savior has been born: He is Christ, the Lord. You'll find Him wrapped in strips of cloth, lying in a manger."

Right at that moment, a multitude of other angels appeared. They praised God and said, "Glory to God in the highest." This must have been one huge birthday celebration! *If you were planning Jesus' birthday celebration, what would you do for His party?*

After the angels left the shepherds and returned to heaven, the shepherds hurried to see the baby. They found Him with Mary and Joseph just as the angel had said. Afterward, the shepherds told everyone they could about the Savior being born, and all who heard the news were amazed.

Mary thought deeply about everything that had happened. She treasured every detail in her heart. *What is a memory in your life that you treasure and love?*

? QUESTIONS

- In what ways was Mary humble?
- God had great purposes for Mary. He has purposes for you, too. What do you think one of yours is?
- What is beautiful about Mary's heart?

✛ PRAYER

Lord, help us be humble and caring like Mary was. You did great things through Mary, an ordinary person. We're excited to see what You do through us. Thank You for giving us the best Christmas gift ever: Jesus. In Jesus' name, amen.

⚑ DAUGHTERS IN ACTION

Materials: Gift bags, small gifts

This week, practice being humble like Mary. Explain to your daughter that humility means thinking about others before yourself and not being showy. You can practice this by giving in secret through Ring and Runs! Make small gift bags including items such as stickers, bath bombs, or baked cookies. Designate several families to receive the gift bags. In each bag, include a note sharing why the family is a treasure, but don't sign your names on the note. Sneak up to the front door of each family's home, drop the bag, ring the doorbell, and run!

CREATIVE FUN

Materials: Ingredients to bake a cake, craft supplies, recycled materials

Bake a cake to celebrate Jesus' birthday even if it's not Christmastime! Together, use any craft materials or objects from the recycle bin to create a Nativity scene. Read Luke 2 to decide what to include in your scene.

For the manger, you could use a cardboard box. Small pieces of yarn could be hay in the manger. Use toilet paper tubes or upside-down paper cups for the people. You can paint them or wrap them with felt or fabric from old clothes. When the scene is complete, have fun acting out the account of Jesus' birth and enjoying a slice of birthday cake!

23

GIVING THANKS
—ANNA

(Luke 2)

Words for Your Heart

Now may the God of hope fill you with all joy and peace as you believe in Him so that you may overflow with hope by the power of the Holy Spirit.

ROMANS 15:13

*E*ight days after Mary had her baby, Mary and Joseph named Him Jesus. That was the name the angel had told Mary to give Him. In those days, it was the tradition to present the firstborn son to God at the Temple when the baby was about a month old. This was to show that the child belonged to the Lord. So Mary and Joseph brought Jesus to the Temple in Jerusalem.

An old woman named Anna was always at the temple worshipping God day and night. She had been married for seven years, but then her husband died so she became a widow. Anna was probably sad and lonely at times, but she still prayed and worshipped constantly. *Why do you think it helps to pray when we're feeling sad or lonely?*

There was also a man named Simeon just outside the Temple. He was faithful and righteous. God had promised Simeon that he would see the Messiah before he died. On the day that Mary and Joseph brought Jesus to the Temple, the Holy Spirit urged Simeon to go inside the Temple courts.

Simeon took Jesus into his arms, praised God, and said, "Lord, it has happened just as You promised. I have seen Your salvation. He is a light to all the nations and the glory of Your people."

Mary and Joseph were amazed at what Simeon said. *What would you have asked Mary and Joseph or said to them if you were there?*

When Anna saw Simeon with Jesus, Mary, and Joseph, she came right up to them. *Since Anna loved God, what do you think her reaction was when she finally saw Jesus, the Son of God, in front of her very eyes?*

Anna was a prophetess. *Do you remember three other women who were also prophetesses?* Deborah, Miriam, and Huldah were all prophetesses who shared God's word with others.

Anna was excited about seeing Jesus at the Temple. She immediately gave thanks to God. Then she told the Good News about Jesus to everyone who was looking forward to the Messiah. Just like Simeon, she knew that Jesus was the promised Messiah who came to save people from their sins. She couldn't hold the Good News in—she wanted people everywhere to hear it.

Anna continued loving God and giving thanks even though she had been through something difficult. That can be tough to do, but when we pray to God and praise Him even in the hard times, He will help us. *How can you find your strength and hope in the Lord, even when you are in an uncomfortable or hard situation?*

When Jesus was grown-up, He shared these comforting words: "My peace I give you. . . . Do not let your hearts be troubled and do not be afraid" (John 14:27, NIV). Anna was a great example of a woman who found her hope and peace in the Lord.

 **QUESTIONS**
- How did Anna respond after going through something difficult in her life?
- After seeing Jesus in the Temple, how did Anna show her excitement to others?
- What is beautiful about Anna's heart?

 PRAYER

Lord, help us to be thankful and to find our hope and peace in You during hard times. Help us to share about You with joy just like Anna did. Help us to encourage those who, like Anna, have lost their spouses. Please give them comfort. In Jesus' name, amen.

 DAUGHTERS IN ACTION

Together with your daughter, encourage a widow or widower to have hope in the Lord. Consider making a card with Romans 15:13 on it. Then bring the person a meal, do yard work for them, or simply ask how you can help. Or you can support the spouse of someone deployed in the military or a single mom or dad.

 CREATIVE FUN

Materials: Ice cubes, saucepan, food coloring

Show your daughter that the Trinity (God the Father, God the Son, and God the Holy Spirit) is present in the Bible passage for this devotion. *Jesus* was in the Temple, and Anna couldn't wait to tell people about Him. The *Holy Spirit* urged Simeon into the Temple. And Jesus was dedicated to *God* at the Temple. The following activity is a visual representation of the Trinity—three Persons who make up one Being.

1. Have your daughter take a few ice cubes from the freezer and put them in the saucepan.

2. Turn on the stove and melt the ice cubes. (Only Mom should use the stove.) Point out that the water is the same substance as the ice.

3. Bring the water to a boil. Point out the water turning to steam. Encourage your daughter to notice that the steam is the same substance as the ice and the water.

4. Add various colors of food coloring to the water in the pan to see some neat colors and patterns.

Explain to your daughter that God, Jesus, and the Holy Spirit are the same in essence—they are one God. Similarly, ice, liquid water, and steam are all the same in essence. But Jesus, God, and the Holy Spirit are also three distinct persons, a little like how ice, liquid water, and steam are all distinct.

24

JOY IN JESUS —THE WOMAN AT THE WELL

(John 4)

Words for Your Heart

*My mouth will tell about Your righteousness
and Your salvation all day long.*

PSALM 71:15

*J*esus was traveling from Judea to Galilee and had to pass through Samaria. Samaria was a place most Jewish people avoided. The Jews and the Samaritans believed different things and didn't get along very well. *Whether people are similar to us or different from us, do you know what God says to do?* God says to love one another.

While most Jewish people avoided Samaritans, do you think Jesus did? No! Jesus knew there was a Samaritan woman there who was hurting because of the wrong choices she'd made. This woman had been chasing one thing after another trying to be happy. But none of it was working. Jesus also knows when you're hurting and wants to help you, too. All you have to do is ask Him.

Jesus and His disciples had come to a town in Samaria called Sychar. The disciples went into town to buy food. But Jesus was tired from His journey, so at about noon He stopped and rested by a well, which is a hole in the ground that supplies water. *Why do you think Jesus chose that exact time and place to rest?*

Normally, women would come outside to draw water from the well in the morning and at night when the day was cool. But this woman drew water in the blazing heat of the day. She was probably trying to avoid people so she wouldn't be teased or judged by others. *How do you think the Samaritan woman felt about herself? If you see other kids who are being left out, what can you do to include them?*

Jesus knew when the woman would come to the well, and He was there waiting for her. *What does this tell you about Jesus?* As she approached the well, Jesus asked her to give Him a drink. Jews didn't normally talk with Samaritans, so the woman was surprised and said, "But You're a Jew, and I'm a Samaritan. Why would You ask me for a drink?"

Jesus looked into her eyes and said, "People who drink water from this well will get thirsty again. But anyone who drinks living water from Me won't ever be thirsty. The water I give is a spring of water that gives eternal life."

Jesus wanted her to know that all the things she was chasing wouldn't fill her heart up. But He would fill her heart up forever. The woman said to Him, "Please give me this water so I won't get thirsty again."

Then Jesus told the woman that He knew all about her sinful choices. The woman was surprised He knew since this was the first time she had met Him. But remember that God knows everything.

She answered, "I can see that You're a prophet. We know that the Messiah is coming and will explain all of this to us."

Jesus declared, "I am He." *How do you think she felt when she learned that she was talking to the promised Messiah?*

Before the woman met Jesus by the well, she made sure not to be seen by anyone. But after the woman spent time with Jesus, her heart was full. She left her water jar at the well, and she ran to find people and tell them about Jesus.

After listening to the woman, the people couldn't wait to meet Jesus. Once they had talked with Jesus, they wanted to spend more time with Him, so they asked Him to stay two more days . . . so He did. Then the people said, "Now we know that Jesus is the Savior of the world." Because of the woman's testimony and Jesus' words, many more people became believers.

❓ QUESTIONS

- Why do you think Jesus made time for the woman at the well?
- How did the woman show her joy in Jesus after meeting with Him?
- What is beautiful about the woman at the well's heart?

✝ PRAYER

Jesus, thank You for Your compassion and for spending time with the woman at the well. We pray we would listen to You like she did and tell others about You. Just as You filled her heart, please fill our hearts, too, so we find our joy in You. In Jesus' name, amen.

↪ DAUGHTERS IN ACTION

Practice finding joy in Jesus this week by giving thanks. At the end of the week, sit together in front of the Well of Thanks from the activity below and talk about what you wrote on the bricks.

CREATIVE FUN

Materials: Construction paper or cardstock, scissors, painter's tape, superglue, washable marker, Popsicle sticks, pom-poms

Make a Well of Thanks on your wall at home. To make the well, use four pieces of construction paper or cardstock. You can use different colors to make it more colorful. Turn the paper so it's horizontal and cut it into three long strips. Then cut those three strips in half so you have six rectangles or "bricks." Do this with each piece of paper. Using painter's tape, tape each brick horizontally, making a well shape that's about four bricks wide and six bricks tall. If you like, you can add a "Well of Thanks" label and attach it to the top of your craft with two longer strips of paper, as shown in the illustration above.

To remind yourself that there is joy in Jesus, make a cross out of Popsicle sticks and adhere it to the well. To do this, glue or tape two Popsicle sticks vertically and one horizontally to make a cross; then superglue pom-poms to the cross. Tape the cross to the middle of the well.

Place a washable marker nearby. Throughout the week, write or draw things you're thankful for on the bricks of the well.

25

GOD'S GREATEST GIFT —THE LOVING WOMAN

(Luke 7)

Words for Your Heart

Above all, love each other deeply.

I PETER 4:8, NIV

Simon belonged to a group called the Pharisees. Pharisees were people who followed Jewish law very closely. They thought they could earn God's approval by doing everything right. *Do you think God loves you more if you are the smartest or strongest kid and get most everything right?* No! Jesus' love is a gift, and you are precious to Him.

One day, Simon invited Jesus over to his house for dinner. *If Jesus came to your house, what would you want to cook for Him?*

While Simon and Jesus were at the dining table, a woman who had lived a sinful life came to Simon's house to see Jesus. *Why do you think this woman wanted to see Jesus?*

When the woman saw Jesus, she fell to the ground behind Him, and she began weeping. Her tears fell on Jesus' feet. The woman dried Jesus' feet with her hair, and she poured a bottle of expensive perfume on His feet.

The woman wanted to show Jesus that she loved Him and

needed His grace. Ephesians 2:8 says that God's grace is a gift from Him. *What do we have to do to receive a gift?* All we have to do is open our hands and accept it. All we have to do to receive God's gift of grace is open our hearts to Him. That's exactly what this woman did.

When Simon the Pharisee saw what the woman was doing, he said to himself, "If Jesus really were a prophet, He would know that this woman is a sinner." Simon questioned who Jesus was because Jesus was being kind to this woman.

It was easy for Simon to see that the woman was a sinner. But it was harder for him to see his own sin. The Bible tells us that all people need forgiveness—even people who try very hard to do the right thing all the time like Simon. Instead of focusing on other people's sins, we can pray for God to help us with our own sins. *What is one thing you want the Lord to help you with?*

Jesus knows our thoughts, so He knew what Simon had said to himself. *How do you think Jesus felt about Simon's words?* After Simon had doubted Jesus, Jesus said to him, "When I came to your house today, you didn't provide any water to wash My feet. But this woman wet My feet with her tears, and she dried My feet with her hair. You didn't put oil on My head, but she poured perfume on My feet."

Then Jesus said, "I tell you, her many sins have been forgiven; that's why she loved much." And He said to the woman, "Your faith has saved you. Go in peace."

? QUESTIONS
- What saved the woman?
- What did the woman do to please Jesus that Simon didn't do?
- What is beautiful about the loving woman's heart?

PRAYER

Jesus, help us to love You by spending time with You, just as this woman did. Please help us to realize the areas in which we need to grow rather than being critical of others. Thank You for Your awesome grace. In Jesus' name, amen.

 DAUGHTERS IN ACTION

Materials: Paper, pencil, envelope

On strips of paper, have your daughter write or draw seven ways she can love Jesus this week. Put the strips of paper in an envelope, and choose one to do each day. Some ideas might include writing a prayer to God, going on a "praise walk" where you praise Him for what He's created, writing a note about why you love a family member and putting it in a place where he or she will see it, helping do dishes, reading the Bible, singing a song to God, or making cookies for people who are sometimes overlooked, like the janitor of your school or church.

 CREATIVE FUN

Materials: Small wooden or cardboard box, markers or paint, small mirror, glue, dry-erase marker

This activity reflects what the Lord wants most from us. It's also a great reminder that the Lord loves us.

1. Decorate the outside of the box and write on it: "Open to see the greatest gift you can give to God."

2. Glue the mirror to the inside base of the box. With a dry-erase marker, write "You!" on the mirror. Share it with your family and friends!

26

SUPPORTING JESUS— MARY MAGDALENE, JOANNA, SUSANNA, AND OTHERS

(Luke 8)

Words for Your Heart

By this all people will know that you are My disciples,
if you have love for one another.

JOHN 13:35

$\mathcal{J}$esus traveled to more towns preaching the Good News of the Kingdom of God. *Do you know what the Good News is?* Jesus is the Good News! Our sins separate us from God. But when we repent and trust in Jesus, God forgives our sins so that we can be close to Him. Jesus made a way for us to have a relationship with God now and forever. That's good news!

Jesus' twelve disciples traveled with Him, but they weren't the only ones with Jesus—there were also many women. In those days, it was normal for men to be the ones in important roles instead of women. But Jesus didn't leave out women. He made sure women were part of His ministry because all people matter deeply to Jesus. *If you were one of the people traveling with Jesus, what would you have talked about with Him as you walked along the road together?*

Mary Magdalene was one of the women who walked with Jesus. Jesus had healed her from evil spirits and diseases that were hurting her body and mind. Mary showed her gratefulness to Jesus by supporting and following Him.

How do you think Jesus, the disciples, and these women were able to have food to eat and places to stay along the way? Some people welcomed them into their homes and provided for them, but there were other times they needed to buy food and find places to stay. Mary Magdalene used her own money to help support His ministry.

Joanna was another woman Jesus had healed. Joanna was married to a man named Chuza. He managed Herod's household, which was a really important job. Herod was the ruler of Galilee, and he was an enemy of Jesus. Even though Joanna's husband worked for an enemy of Jesus, Joanna made the brave choice to follow Jesus. *What about Joanna do you think pleased Jesus?*

After Jesus healed Joanna, she never forgot it. Joanna helped support Jesus' work and provided for Him and the others, just as Mary Magdalene did.

Susanna and many other women also supported Jesus. He had healed them all. These women were grateful that Jesus had healed them, and they stayed by His side, helping in any way they could. They were changed by the love of Jesus, and they wanted to help Him and share His love with others, so they provided for Jesus and His followers during their journeys with their own money.

Jesus also wants you to follow Him and share about Him with others because you are special to Him too.

? QUESTIONS

- How did these women show Jesus they were grateful to Him?

- These women supported Jesus' ministry. How can you support Jesus' ministry?
- What is beautiful about these women's hearts?

PRAYER

Jesus, thank You for being the Good News and for healing these women. We are thankful that they cared deeply for You and supported You with their own money. We pray we would always support Your work and tell others about You. In Jesus' name, amen.

DAUGHTERS IN ACTION

Materials: Note cards, pens

Share the Good News with someone by writing a note that includes a verse about Jesus such as John 3:16, John 14:6, or Romans 8:38-39. Express how much Jesus cares for the person. Consider putting the note on a neighbor's front door. Another idea is to pay for someone's order behind you in a drive-thru line. Give the note to the cashier, and ask him or her to give it to the person for whom you paid.

CREATIVE FUN

Materials: Craft pipe cleaners, a stick, large bowl, whisk or mixing spoon, 4 cups very warm water, ½ cup sugar, ½ cup dish soap

This simple bubble activity will show your daughter how spending time with Jesus, as these women did, allows God's love to reach others. In this activity, you and your daughter will dip a pipe-cleaner wand (representing your heart) into the bubble solution (representing Jesus). When you wave the wand, lots of bubbles (representing the love of Jesus) will spread around you.

1. To make a wand, shape the top of the pipe cleaner into a circle, and twist the ends of the pipe cleaner to the end of a stick. Make sure the circle will fit into the bowl you mix the bubble solution in.

2. Mix the very warm water with the sugar until it dissolves.

3. Add the dish soap to the mixture and whisk it together, but don't overmix it.

4. Dip the wand into the bubble solution.

5. As you wave the wand around you, it will create lots of big bubbles.

27

BEAUTIFUL FAITH
—THE DESPERATE WOMAN

(Mark 5)

Words for Your Heart

I am the light of the world. Anyone who follows Me will never
walk in the darkness but will have the light of life.

JOHN 8:12

*J*esus continued traveling to different towns by boat, teaching people about the Kingdom of God. A crowd stood along the shore, waiting to spend time with Jesus. *If you could spend the day with Jesus, what would you want to do together?*

At the same time, a twelve-year-old girl had become very sick. Jairus, the girl's father, knew he had to find Jesus for his daughter to be healed. Making his way through the crowd, Jairus found Jesus and fell at His feet. Jairus begged Him, "My daughter is dying. Please come and heal her so that she will live." *What does this show about Jairus' faith in Jesus?*

Jesus agreed to go with Jairus. On the way, the crowd pressed into Jesus because they all wanted to be close to Him. There was a woman in the crowd who had been sick for twelve years. No one had been able to heal her.

The woman had spent all of her money going to different doctors, but instead of getting better, she got worse. She had been sick for so long, and she was desperate to be healed. The woman heard that Jesus was in the crowd, so she squeezed through to find Him. She had to see Him. *Do you think Jesus could help her?*

As soon as the woman saw Jesus, she came up behind Him. She said to herself, "If I just touch Jesus' clothes, I'll be healed." She had walked in darkness and pain for so long. She longed for Jesus, the Light of the World, to shine His healing light on her.

She stretched out her hand and touched Jesus' robe. Immediately she was healed.

Even with so many people crowding around Him, Jesus knew that someone had touched Him and had been healed. Jesus was on His way somewhere, but this woman needed Him, so He stopped and made time for her. He said to her, "Daughter, because you believed, you have been healed. Go in peace. You won't suffer anymore."

While Jesus was speaking, a man from Jairus' house came and said, "Your daughter has died. There's no need to bother Jesus anymore." *What do you think Jesus did?* Jesus ignored what the man said. He looked at Jairus and said, "Don't be afraid. Just believe."

Jesus went to Jairus' home. Many people were gathered at the home weeping because the girl had died. "Why are you crying?" Jesus asked them. "The girl isn't dead. She's just asleep."

The people laughed at Jesus. They didn't understand that Jesus is God and that He can do anything. *How do you think Jesus responded to the people laughing at Him?*

Jesus didn't let these people stop Him. He made all of them leave the house except for His disciples Peter, James, and John, and also the girl's mom and dad. *Why do you think Jesus made everyone leave the house except for her parents and some disciples?*

Jesus went to the little girl, took her hand, and said, "My child, get up!"

At once, the girl got up and walked around the room. She was alive again! *What do you think the girl did after Jesus healed her?*

The disciples and the girl's mom and dad were amazed that Jesus healed the girl. Then Jesus told the family to get her something to eat. Jesus cared about the girl's big and small needs. He also cares deeply about the big and small needs in your life.

? QUESTIONS
- How did the desperate woman show her faith in Jesus?
- When did a busy person make time for you? How did that make you feel?
- What is beautiful about the desperate woman's heart?

✝ PRAYER
Jesus, thank You for healing the desperate woman and the twelve-year-old girl and for caring so much about them. Help us have faith in You like the desperate woman did. Please be with those who are lonely or sick right now and give them hope and healing. In Jesus' name, amen.

⚑ DAUGHTERS IN ACTION
Materials: Gift items

If you know a child who is in the hospital, purchase a gift for him or her. You can order it online to be sent directly to the child if the hospital is not allowing visitors.

If you don't know a child staying at the hospital, you can contact the child life program at the children's hospital to ask about their policy. Some hospitals allow you to bring unwrapped, new gifts for the patients and will meet you outside the hospital to get them. Some hospitals also have wish lists so you can directly order items online to be sent there. You can also ask if they have specific needs. Some of the items they usually need (new in package) are stuffed animals, lap games, books, play dough, and light-up toys or glitter wands.

 CREATIVE FUN

Materials: A flashlight

Explain to your daughter that the desperate woman needed Jesus, the Light of the World, to heal her. To illustrate this truth, hold a flashlight in your hand that isn't turned on and try to walk through a very dark room (slowly, so you don't hurt yourself). Explain to your daughter that just as it's hard to walk through the dark room, it's hard to walk through life without Jesus being our light. Now turn on the flashlight and walk through the dark room. When we ask Jesus to be our light, we shine for Him, and it's so much easier to find our way!

28

MARY SITS WITH JESUS —MARY AND MARTHA

(Luke 10)

Words for Your Heart

I am the vine; you are the branches. The one who remains in Me and I in him produces much fruit.

JOHN 15:5

*J*esus and His disciples visited Bethany, where two sisters named Martha and Mary lived. (This was a different Mary than Jesus' mother). Martha welcomed Jesus to her home, and Mary sat at His feet and listened to Him.

As Mary and Jesus sat there together, what do you think they talked about? Maybe Jesus told Mary about His great love for us, or maybe He told her one of the parables about the Kingdom of God.

While Jesus talked with Mary, Martha was very busy. She was concerned with all the things that needed to be done for His visit. Maybe Martha was preparing dinner or cleaning up the house. While Martha was busy working around the house, she got upset about something. *What do you think Martha was upset about?*

Martha came to Jesus and said, "Lord, don't You care that

Mary is leaving all the work to me? Tell Mary to help me!" *How was Martha feeling?* Martha had become frustrated and annoyed. *Is there a time you felt like Martha and were doing most of the work or cleaning up?* It can be easy to be angry when others aren't helping. But Jesus wanted Martha to think about something else— something that was more important than who was doing the most work.

How do you think Jesus responded to Martha being annoyed at her sister? Jesus said to her, "Martha, Martha, you are worried and upset about all of these details. But there's only one thing that's important. Mary chose the right thing, and it won't be taken away from her." *What was the one thing that was important?* Mary chose to spend time with Jesus. But Martha was so busy doing her work that she didn't spend time with Jesus, who was a very special guest. *What do you think Jesus cared most about—a clean house and a perfect dinner or spending time with the two sisters?* Jesus loved Mary and Martha, and He wanted to spend time talking with them.

Jesus didn't yell at Martha, and He didn't ignore how she felt. Jesus gently told Martha what really mattered. We can always tell Jesus exactly how we feel. He's big enough to handle all our thoughts and emotions. Jesus never changes. He is always there for us.

Jesus talked about the importance of spending time with Him in John 15:5. He said, "I am the vine; you are the branches. The one who remains in Me and I in him produces much fruit." On a grapevine, the branches sprout out from the vine, and healthy branches produce lots of fruit. Jesus is saying that if we spend time with Him, then we will do many good things that honor Him and help others. *What are some examples of good fruit you think Mary might have had after spending time with Jesus?*

 ## QUESTIONS
- What did Mary do that pleased Jesus?
- What is one way you can be like Mary?
- What is beautiful about Mary's heart?

 ## PRAYER
Lord, during the day when we're busy, remind us to slow down and spend time with You so we can produce much fruit and be more like You. In Jesus' name, amen.

DAUGHTERS IN ACTION

Help your daughter create a habit of spending time with God daily. One way to do this is to set a reminder on your phone to pray together each day. Below is a prayer guide based on the Lord's Prayer in Luke 11. You may want to write it out in a journal each day to guide your prayer times. However, prayer is just talking to God from your heart, so you don't have to follow the guide. You can pray in one sentence, in silence, together, or by yourself. What matters is spending time with God.

Praise: Tell God why He's awesome and why you love Him.

His Will: Ask God to have His will and way in your life.

Ask: Pray for yourself and others, asking God to meet your needs.

Forgiveness: Tell God ways you've been unloving to Him and others, and ask for forgiveness. Ask the Lord to help you forgive others and to always seek Him first.

Thanks: Tell God what you're thankful for and thank Him for hearing your prayer.

 ## CREATIVE FUN

Materials: Colored paper, crayons or markers, pen, tape, scissors

Draw a picture together of you, your daughter, and Jesus sitting together on a vine, or simply write your names and Jesus' name on a piece of paper and decorate it with a vine. Write John 15:5 on the picture and tape it to the wall. Cut branches from paper and tape them to the wall so they're connected to the vine in the picture. Then cut out twenty large grapes and put them in an envelope. Tape the envelope to the wall. Every time you catch someone in your family showing fruit by loving God and others, write it on a grape and tape it to a branch. Go and bear much fruit this week!

29

MARTHA CHOOSES FAITH —MARTHA AND MARY

(John 11)

Words for Your Heart

With God all things are possible.

MATTHEW 19:26

A long time after Jesus visited Mary and Martha, their brother, Lazarus, became very sick. Jesus was in Jerusalem, so the two sisters sent word to Him that Lazarus wasn't doing well. When Jesus got their message, He said, "The purpose of this illness is not death. It is for God's glory."

Jesus loved Mary, Martha, and Lazarus, but He didn't hurry to be with Lazarus. Instead, Jesus waited. And Lazarus died. *Why do you think Jesus waited to go?*

The siblings lived in Bethany, which was only about two miles from Jerusalem, so many people came from Jerusalem to comfort the sisters. When Jesus arrived, Lazarus had been in the tomb for four days.

Martha heard Jesus was coming, so she went out to meet Him,

but Mary stayed at home. *What did Martha do differently this time than she did the last time Jesus visited?* Martha made sure to go straight to Jesus this time when He arrived.

Martha said to Jesus, "Lord, Lazarus wouldn't have died if You were here." Martha was sad and frustrated because Jesus wasn't there in time. She shared her honest thoughts with Him. *Why do you think Jesus wants us to share our honest thoughts with Him?* Even though the Lord already knows your heart, He loves hearing from you because He cares for you.

In her pain, hurt, and sadness, Martha still had faith and said to Jesus, "But even now, I'm sure that God will give You anything You ask." Even though Martha was very sad, she believed that Jesus could do anything. *Do you also think Jesus could heal Lazarus?*

Jesus said to Martha, "I am the resurrection and the life. Anyone who believes in Me will live, even though he dies. Do you believe this?"

Martha said, "Yes, Lord. I believe that You are the Messiah, the Son of God, the One we've waited for."

Jesus asked Martha to go get Mary. Martha did as Jesus asked, and Mary hurried to Jesus. The people who were comforting Mary followed her.

When Mary saw Jesus, she fell at His feet. Just like Martha, Mary said, "Lord, if You'd been here, Lazarus wouldn't have died." *How do you think Jesus reacted to Mary's sadness about her brother dying?* When Jesus saw Mary and the others weeping, He cried with them. *Why do you think Jesus cried?*

Jesus went to the cave where Lazarus was buried. There was a stone laid across the entrance. Jesus told the people to remove the stone. Jesus looked up and said, "Father, thank You for hearing Me." Then Jesus called in a loud voice, "Lazarus, come out!" *What do you think happened?* Lazarus came out of the cave. He was alive!

Earlier, when Lazarus had died, Mary and Martha didn't understand why Jesus waited to come, but Jesus knew more than they knew. He knew that God would be glorified when He raised Lazarus from the dead. When you don't understand things in your life, you can have faith that God is in charge and that God knows and understands more than you do. You can trust that God's ways are always best.

? QUESTIONS
- Why do you think Martha chose to spend time with Jesus instead of staying busy like she did last time?
- When you are sad, how can you still choose to have faith like Martha?
- What is beautiful about Martha's heart?

✠ PRAYER
Father, help us be honest about what's on our hearts and help us to have faith like Martha, even when we don't understand everything. In Jesus' name, amen.

⚑ DAUGHTERS IN ACTION
Materials: Note cards, pen, a small reward

Only Mom should read this.

Make a scavenger hunt for your daughter to explain what faith is. Tell her that there is a reward at the end. BEFORE your daughter begins the hunt, ask her if she believes there is a reward even though she hasn't seen it yet. Tell her, "That's what faith is—believing even when you don't see it."

1. Write clues on note cards. An example of the first clue could be *This is where you have sweet dreams at night.* Clue 2 could be something like *This is where you'll find cold items that are yummy to your tummy.* Make a handful of other clues. In the final note, consider sharing something that you love about your daughter.

2. Put all the clues in the correct places. Clue 1 will be given to her when you start and clue 2 should be on her bed. Clue 3 should be on the fridge, and so on. As she figures out a clue, she'll head to that place to find the next one and will continue until she reaches the final note that has the reward written on it.

3. Some reward ideas you could write on the last note might be to bake a cake together, bake soft pretzels, or go out together for one of your daughter's favorite treats.

CREATIVE FUN

Materials: A bedsheet

When things didn't make sense to Mary and Martha, they chose to have faith in Jesus. In the same way, we don't always understand everything in our lives, but we can have faith that God sees more than we do and can bring good out of the situation.

Prepare a performance to illustrate this spiritual truth during a family talent show. This act will look confusing because there's more going on behind the sheet that they can't see.

1. Lie down on your back on the floor.

2. Have your daughter gently sit on your stomach facing your feet.

3. Cover your daughter's legs and your head with a sheet (making sure you can still breathe). It will appear that your "daughter's legs" are very long and she will appear very flexible when she does "stretches."

4. Play some fun music as your daughter does silly exercises and dance moves. For example, your daughter can attempt to stretch and touch your toes. You can swing your legs up into a "V" so your daughter appears extra flexible. Keep doing silly things with your legs while she moves her arms. Ask someone to record it to see how hilarious it looks!

30

A WALK OF FAITH —THE BENT-OVER WOMAN

(Luke 13)

Words for Your Heart

Let us run with endurance the race that lies before us,
keeping our eyes on Jesus.

HEBREWS 12:1-2

*T*here was a woman who was completely bent over for eighteen years. She couldn't stand up straight. If you can, walk across the room totally bent over at the waist. That's the way she had to walk all the time.

It probably took a lot of effort for this woman to get from one place to another. However, the woman still came to the synagogue, where people worshipped God. Jesus was teaching at the synagogue on the Sabbath. *Imagine going to church one day and finding out Jesus was the one preaching—how do you think you would react?*

As Jesus was teaching, he noticed the woman. This woman had a disability that could be seen—she was completely bent over. Sometimes kids have disabilities we can see, such as those who rely on a wheelchair, but sometimes kids have disabilities we can't see, such as not being able to hear. These kids want to be treated with kindness, just like you. *When you are around a kid with a disability, what is a way you can be kind to him or her?* Just waving, saying hi, or asking the kid to join you can make that person feel included and cared about.

What do you think Jesus did when He saw the bent-over woman? As soon as Jesus saw the woman, He called her forward. With every step, the woman mostly saw the ground because of her bent back. Every move was probably painful, but she wanted to be close to Jesus. Once she came forward, Jesus said, "Woman, you are set free from your illness." Then Jesus put His hands on her, and she immediately straightened up and praised God. *How do you think the bent-over woman felt being able to finally stand up straight after eighteen years?*

While Jesus has healed many people, it's difficult when someone who's sick doesn't get better. We may not understand God's ways, but we can take comfort that in the good times and hard times, God is our greatest hope. God is always with us, and nothing can ever separate us from His love.

The synagogue leader was angry that Jesus healed the bent-over woman. *Do you know why?* He was angry because Jesus healed her on the Sabbath, which by law was a day of rest. But Jesus is the Lord God. He knew that healing this woman was the right thing to do. Jesus knew that it is right to do good on the Sabbath.

Jesus said the synagogue leader and some of the other people were hypocrites—that means they said they believed one thing, but they did something else. Jesus told them how they had not rested on the Sabbath.

Then Jesus said, "Should this woman, whom Satan has hurt for eighteen long years, not be set free because it's the Sabbath day?" Satan is God's enemy, but we don't need to worry because God is far bigger and more powerful than him.

When Jesus said this, the people who questioned Him were embarrassed. But the people who supported Jesus were in awe of all the wonderful things He did.

The amazing things Jesus did didn't stop there. One of Jesus' disciples, John, tells us that "there are also many other things that Jesus did, which, if they were written one by one, I suppose not even the world itself could contain the books that would be written" (John 21:25).

? QUESTIONS

- Why do you think Jesus called the bent-over woman forward instead of walking to her?
- How did the woman show faith?
- What is beautiful about the bent-over woman's heart?

✝ PRAYER

We praise You, Lord, for healing the bent-over woman. Help us to have faith in You and to praise You like she did. Thank You for caring about someone other people might have ignored. Help us do the same. In Jesus' name, amen.

▷ DAUGHTERS IN ACTION

If visitors are allowed, visit the elderly in a nursing home. You can bring books to read to them, puzzles to do, or a list of questions to ask them to learn about their lives. If you're unable to visit, you can mail encouraging cards to the nursing home residents. Or you can reach out to elderly neighbors by asking them if they need help around the house or would like a visit. You can also make cards for them to brighten their day.

CREATIVE FUN

Materials: Cardstock, crayons or markers, scissors, brad fasteners

On cardstock, draw pictures of Jesus and the bent-over woman. Cut out each person. Cut the figure of the bent-over woman in half. Overlap the top half of the woman with the bottom half of her so there is just enough space to push a brad fastener through both pieces. Then you can rotate her bending over and straightening up. Use the figures to act out the Bible passage.

31

NOT GIVING UP
—THE PERSISTENT WIDOW

(Luke 18)

Words for Your Heart

Rejoice always! Pray constantly. Give thanks in everything,
for this is God's will for you in Christ Jesus.

I THESSALONIANS 5:16-18

*J*esus continued teaching people in different towns about how to know God and seek His Kingdom. *Why do you think Jesus went to different places to share about the Kingdom of God?* When Jesus taught, He often used parables, or stories. *Why do you think Jesus taught with stories?* One day while Jesus was traveling, He told His disciples a parable about praying always and not giving up. It went like this:

There was once a widow who was treated unfairly. *When someone treats you unfairly, what is something you can do about it?* The widow was upset and went to the judge. She begged him to give her justice and to be fair. But the judge refused to help her. *What do you think she did?* The woman was persistent, which means she didn't give up.

She kept asking the judge for help over and over again.
He finally agreed to help her and granted her justice
because of her persistence.

In this parable, Jesus wanted His disciples to understand the importance of continuing to come to God, no matter what, just as this woman kept going to the judge. Even though life was hard for her and she was treated unfairly, she didn't give up. *When is a time you persisted in something and didn't give up?*

When we talk to God each day about what's on our minds and hearts, we are being persistent in prayer. When you have a tough day or a great day, God wants you to pray. You can talk to Him anytime and anywhere, and He is always there for you.

After sharing the parable, Jesus asked His disciples, "Won't God listen and bring justice to His people when they call out to Him day and night?" Jesus is saying that God wants you to come to Him in prayer, and He promises to answer you. God might answer your prayer exactly how you want Him to, or He might answer it differently. God's ways are higher than our ways. We can't always understand God, but we can trust Him because He cares for us.

Why do you think God wants you to come to Him in prayer? Just as you talk and spend time with your family and friends because you love them, God wants to spend time with you because He loves you and wants a relationship with you. When you are persistent in prayer, another beautiful thing happens—you get to know the Lord better and your heart becomes more like His.

❓ QUESTIONS

- What do you think helped the persistent widow not to give up?

- What is something you want to pray about persistently?
- What is beautiful about the persistent widow's heart?

 PRAYER

Lord, we are thankful that we can always pray to You and that You always hear and answer us. Help us to be persistent in prayer, just like the persistent widow. In Jesus' name, amen.

 DAUGHTERS IN ACTION

Practice being persistent in prayer with your daughter. Find a journal or notebook that can be a mother-daughter prayer journal. Each day this week, write the day's date at the top of a page. Have your daughter write something she wants you to pray about. Sometime during the day, write a prayer for her using her request as a guide for your prayer. Then write something you'd like her to pray about for you. Leave the journal in a special spot so you both know where to find it.

After this week, you can continue using the prayer journal. Or you can extend the activity and simply write notes to each other in the journal when something's on your heart. This is a great way to connect with your daughter.

 CREATIVE FUN

Materials: Markers, photograph of you and your daughter, glue, stickers, self-stick decorations

Have fun decorating your mother-daughter prayer journal together. You can write 1 Thessalonians 5:16-18 on the front. You can also glue a picture of the two of you on the front to make it meaningful. Write the starting date on the journal so you'll always remember when you did this activity together.

32

GIVING EVERYTHING
—THE POOR WIDOW

(Mark 12)

Words for Your Heart

God loves a cheerful giver.

2 CORINTHIANS 9:7

*L*arge crowds gathered around Jesus at the Temple. Many loved listening to Him teach, but there were some leaders who didn't. They didn't understand who Jesus was, and they thought He was teaching things that were wrong. These men wanted to get rid of Jesus because they were jealous of the attention He was getting and how He amazed the crowds. *Do you think that stopped Jesus?* No! Jesus kept on teaching!

Many people at the Temple asked Jesus questions so they could know Him better. But others wanted to trap Him with a tricky question so He could be arrested. *Do you think Jesus knew if people asked Him questions to try to trick Him or because they cared?* Yes! Jesus is wise, and He also knows our thoughts. Jesus had wise answers for every kind of question.

Jesus told the people to watch out for people who were unkind to widows and for those who said long prayers just to show off. *Why do you think these things bothered Jesus?* Jesus wants us to care for widows and to pray with pure, loving hearts rather than trying to impress others. Jesus knew a poor widow was on her way to the Temple, which might have been just the reason He was teaching about this.

After teaching, Jesus sat down opposite the Temple treasury. This was where money was collected for the Temple. *What do you think you would do if you saw Jesus sitting in church when you got there?*

Jesus watched many rich people throw in large amounts of money. Then He saw the poor widow walking toward the treasury. The woman gripped her only two copper coins, worth less than a penny. She needed the money, but she also wanted to give to God. *What do you think the woman did with her only two coins?* She put all the money she had inside the Temple treasury for the Lord.

How do you think Jesus felt about what this woman did? Right away, Jesus called His disciples over to Him. Jesus said, "This poor widow has given more than all the others. They have lots of money, and they gave some of it. But this woman only had a little bit of money. She gave all the money she had to live on."

Even though the amount she gave didn't seem like much to others, it was a lot to her because it was all she had. *Did the widow announce to everyone what she did?* She gave quietly out of her love for the Lord. Jesus was so pleased that He told His disciples about it. He also notices when we give out of love for Him and others.

Make two fists with your hands as tightly as you can. If we hold on tightly to our things like this, there is no room in our closed hands to give or receive anything, and it can make us selfish and unhappy. Now, open your hands. The Lord wants us to have open hands with our things so we can more easily give and receive. *What do you think it means to be openhanded?* When we are open to giving like the poor widow was, and don't hold on to our things so tightly, we can experience more of the Kingdom of God and we can love like Jesus loved.

? QUESTIONS
- How did the poor widow give more if the rich gave a larger amount of money?
- What are ways you can show your love for God besides giving money?
- What is beautiful about the poor widow's heart?

PRAYER

Lord, we want to seek You first and give out of love like the poor widow did. Help us to have open hands and an open heart to give. In Jesus' name, amen.

 DAUGHTERS IN ACTION

Think of ways to go above and beyond with loving God and others. Here are some ideas:

1. Your daughter could give away one of her favorite toys to the church or a shelter.

2. Each of you could make a family member's bed or help with a chore without being asked. But don't say anything to them about it so you can give in secret.

3. If you have long hair, you could cut it and donate it to a place that makes wigs for sick children.

4. You could make a card and cupcakes for first responders. Thank them for going above and beyond serving the community. (Save some batter to make a crazy cupcake for each of you with fun ingredients such as gummy bears, sprinkles, or chocolate chips.)

 CREATIVE FUN

Materials: Cardstock, scissors, yarn, tape, 2 T-shirts, blanket

Create a skit about giving with upside-down chin faces to get the giggles going because "God loves a cheerful giver" (2 Corinthians 9:7).

1. From cardstock, cut out a nose and eyes, or use googly eyes.

2. Tape yarn for "hair" to the bottom of your chins and tape eyes between your lips and the yarn hair, leaving room for a nose.

3. Tape the nose between the eyes and your bottom lip.

4. Get two T-shirts and a blanket and scoot to the end of a bed, lying on your backs. Tilt your chins toward the ceiling.

5. Cover your real hair, eyes, and nose, with a T-shirt and cover your bodies, up to your neck, with the blanket so only your mouths and chins show.

6. Now, create a skit! In the first scene, one person can act selfish, not wanting to share. The other person can be extra dramatic and react sadly about it. Then, in scene 2, the selfish person can change her mind and be happy to give to the other person. The other person should overreact again, but this time with a joyful heart because the first person chose to give! You can also make silly expressions and sing funny songs. Just make sure you have someone to record it all to see how hilarious it looks!

33

THE POWER OF LOVE
—THE WOMEN AT
THE CROSS

(Matthew 26–27)

Words for Your Heart

For God so loved the world that he gave his one and only Son,
that whoever believes in him shall not perish but have eternal life.

JOHN 3:16, NIV

*F*or three years Jesus had taught about the kingdom of God. He
had healed people who were sick, blind, or deaf. He'd even raised
people from the dead. Everything Jesus did showed His power
and His love for people. Jesus showed that He was truly the Son
of God.

Jesus had taught that He would die for the sins of the world
and He would rise again. It was almost time for this all to happen.
Jesus was feeling sad and troubled, so He went to a garden with His
disciples, and then He went off by Himself and prayed earnestly.

After praying, Jesus returned to His disciples. A large crowd
holding torches and lanterns, and armed with swords, had come
to arrest Him. When the men stepped forward to arrest Jesus, one
of His disciples, Peter, lifted his sword to protect Jesus. The servant
of the high priest was injured.

Jesus healed the man and told Peter to put the sword away. Jesus said, "If I needed help, I could call on my Father and He would send twelve legions of angels to save Me." *One legion of Roman soldiers was about six thousand soldiers, so about how many angels would twelve legions be?* God would have sent seventy-two thousand angels if Jesus had asked for help!

But Jesus didn't ask God to stop His arrest. Instead, Jesus said, "It must happen in this way so the Scriptures will be fulfilled." Isaiah 53, written six hundred years before Jesus was born, revealed that the Messiah would die for our sins and rise again. Now this was about to happen. *How do you think Isaiah knew Jesus would die and rise again over six hundred years before it happened?* Isaiah was a prophet who shared messages from God with the people.

The soldiers arrested Jesus, and His disciples fled. Early in the morning, the leaders decided to crucify Jesus, which means He would die on the Cross.

Who do you think stood near Jesus at the Cross to support Him? The Bible tells us that many women were there. The book of John tells us that Jesus' mother, Mary, was there. She wanted to be close to her Son so He would feel supported by her presence. She must have been filled with so many emotions as she thought about the birth and life of her Son.

The book of Matthew tells us that Mary Magdalene was there, too, along with the mother of James and Joseph, and the mother of Zebedee's sons. Many of these women had followed Jesus from Galilee to take care of His needs. The women watched from a distance as Jesus died on the Cross.

It would have been really easy for these women not to show up during such a difficult time, but people who love you show up even when it's tough. *Who has shown up for you during a tough time? Is there someone you can be there for who's going through a difficult time?*

While it was difficult for these women to see Jesus experience that pain on the Cross, it was even more difficult for Jesus. But His love for us and for God strengthened Him. Jesus knew we needed a way to be forgiven so we could be with God forever. Jesus took our sins upon Himself when He died on the Cross. *What does that say about His love for you?*

? QUESTIONS
- How did these women show Jesus that they truly loved Him?
- Why do you think Jesus wanted these women as a part of His ministry?
- What is beautiful about these women's hearts?

✝ PRAYER
Lord, we are thankful that these women cared so well for Your needs and were by Your side during such a difficult time. Help us not to just tell friends and family we care, but also to show them we care. Thank You for loving us so much that You gave Your life for us. In Jesus' name, amen.

▷ DAUGHTERS IN ACTION
Materials: Paper towels, scissors, casserole dish, permanent marker, washable marker

Together, think through some ways that you've sinned—ways that you have not loved God or others or ways that you've made poor choices. Pray and ask God for forgiveness. Thank Him for loving you so much that He made a way for you to be forgiven.

Then tear off a sheet of paper towel and cut it into two rectangles so they can each fit into a casserole dish. With a PERMANENT marker, draw a really big heart on each of your rectangles. Then, with a WASHABLE marker, write the sins you came up with inside the heart you drew. Keep the rectangles for the *Creative Fun* activity in the next devotion.

CREATIVE FUN

Materials: Gift bag, art supplies, small gift items

The women in this Bible passage supported Jesus during a difficult time. This showed their love for Him. You can show love for others by creating a "Brighten Up" gift bag to give to a friend who has a bad day or is sick. Jesus says that when you care for those in need, you are caring for Him as well (Matthew 25:40), so this is a great way to care for a friend and for Jesus at the same time. Write a Bible verse on the gift bag and include a fun notepad, some markers or colored pencils, play dough, a coloring book or craft, bath bombs, and any other items that might brighten someone's day. Have fun decorating the bag. If you can't think of a friend to give the bag to this week, hold on to it until someone comes to mind.

34

HE HAS RISEN!
—THE THREE MARYS, SALOME,
JOANNA, AND OTHERS

(Matthew 27–28, Luke 23–24)

Words for Your Heart

I am the way, the truth, and the life.

No one comes to the Father except through Me.

JOHN 14:6

*A*ll the women who had come with Jesus from Galilee were heartbroken. Jesus had suffered, and now He was dead. With tear-filled eyes, they watched Joseph, who was a rich man and a follower of Jesus, along with a Pharisee named Nicodemus, wrap Jesus' body in a linen cloth. Then Joseph and Nicodemus put Jesus' body in a tomb, which was a cave carved out of a hill.

The Pharisees, the chief priests, and Pontius Pilate, the governor, remembered that Jesus had said He would rise in three days. They ordered guards to seal the tomb with a stone and to guard it day and night. These leaders didn't believe Jesus would rise. They were afraid the disciples would try to steal Jesus' body from the cave and say that He'd risen when He really hadn't. *Do you think Jesus rose like He said He would?*

Today people usually bring flowers when someone dies, but in those days people showed their love and respect by preparing spices to care for the body.

These brave, caring women not only took care of Jesus during His life, but also after He died. They went home and prepared the spices they needed to care for Jesus. But they had to wait before they could return to the tomb because the Sabbath had begun and the Sabbath was a day of rest. When the Sabbath was over, they left just after sunrise with the spices. *Why do you think they left so early to see Jesus?*

Guards were watching the tomb to make sure it was secure. But suddenly there was a violent earthquake, and an angel came down from heaven. He rolled the stone away and sat on it. The angel looked like lightning, and his clothes were white like snow. *What do you think the guards did when they felt the earthquake and saw the angel?*

The guards shook and froze in fear! The angel turned to the women and said, "Don't be scared. I know you're looking for Jesus. But He's not here. He has risen, just like He said He would."

The angel told them to look in the tomb for Jesus' body. The women discovered that the angel was right—Jesus was no longer in the tomb!

Filled with fear and joy, the women hurried to tell the disciples what they had seen.

When the women left, the guards told the chief priests what had happened. The leaders gave the soldiers a lot of money and said to tell people that Jesus' disciples stole the body. The leaders thought they could lie to stop the truth from coming out. But truth always prevails—nothing would stop Jesus.

As the women ran to the disciples, a man stopped them and said, "Greetings." It was Jesus!

These women were the first ones to see Jesus after He had risen! The women fell at His feet and worshipped Him. They were overjoyed that Jesus was alive! *What would you have done if you were the first one to see Jesus after He had risen?*

Jesus stayed with His followers for forty days. He told them that

He would be going away, and that after He left they would receive the gift of the Holy Spirit. Then Jesus was taken into heaven.

After this, Jesus' followers, including Mary, the mother of Jesus, Jesus' brothers, and the other women, met together and prayed constantly.

 ## QUESTIONS

- Why do you think Jesus chose to appear to these women first after he had risen, before anyone else?
- How did these women show their loyalty and love for Jesus time after time?
- What is beautiful about these women's hearts?

✞ PRAYER

Your daughter may never have had the opportunity to make a personal commitment to Jesus Christ. If this is an appropriate time for that discussion, you can share these words with your daughter:

"If you want to follow Jesus and be with Him always, you can tell Him in a prayer like this one: *I'm so thankful, Lord, that these women chose to follow You and believe in You. I also believe that You died on the Cross and rose to give me life forever with You. Please forgive me for my sins, come into my life, and help me to always follow You. In Jesus' name, amen.*" If your daughter prayed this prayer, take a picture of both of you, print it out, and write the date on the back. Keep it in your Bible to remember this treasured moment of believing in Jesus!

If your daughter is not ready for this conversation or if your daughter has already committed her life to God, you can pray: *Lord, the way You loved the women in this Bible passage is awesome. The way they loved You is awesome too. Please keep speaking to our hearts so that we can know You better. I pray our relationships with You would grow. In Jesus' name, amen.*

DAUGHTERS IN ACTION

Materials: Two sticks, twine or string

Help your daughter find two sticks outside—one should be shorter than the other. Use twine, string, or a rubber band to tie them together to form a cross. After you make the cross, give thanks to Jesus for dying and rising three days later to forgive us of our sins so we can be with Him forever. This is the Good News we celebrate on Easter! You'll use the cross in the next activity.

 CREATIVE FUN

Materials: Praise music, casserole dish, the paper towels you wrote on last week, water, the cross you made in the Daughters in Action activity

Listen to a fun praise song to celebrate Jesus' resurrection as you do this activity!

1. Fill a casserole dish halfway with water.

2. Read the sins you wrote on one of the paper towels last week. Then submerge it completely into the water.

3. The image of the heart will stay, but the sins will become blurry. With the cross you made, push down on the sins and watch them disappear! Explain that this is what happens to our sins when we ask Jesus to forgive us. He washes them away.

4. Thank God for forgiving all your sins. This is Good News to celebrate!

35

CARING FOR THE POOR—TABITHA

(Acts 9)

Words for Your Heart

It is more blessed to give than to receive.

ACTS 20:35

*A*fter Jesus rose from the dead and went to heaven, Jesus' disciples shared the Good News about Him. More and more people were believing in Jesus, and the churches were growing.

Peter, one of Jesus' first disciples, went to visit the believers in Lydda. While Peter was there, he met a man who hadn't walked for eight years. Peter said to the man, "Jesus Christ heals you. Get up." Immediately the man stood—he was healed! All the people there saw what happened, and they believed in Jesus.

One of Jesus' disciples was living nearby in a town called Joppa. Her name was Tabitha, and she was also known as Dorcas. *If you could pick a second name to go by, what would you choose?* Tabitha followed the Lord's two greatest commandments. *Do you remember them?* An easy way to remember is to stretch both arms up and say, "Love God" and then point both arms in opposite directions and say, "Love others." Now you try it!

Tabitha loved God and others by always doing good and helping the poor. *In what ways do you think she might have helped the poor?* The Bible says that we honor God when we take care of others. *Why do you think this honors God?* All we have has been given to us by God. He wants us to love others well with what we have, like Tabitha did. Caring for people by seeing a need and filling it is an example of what a follower of Jesus does. This is one way we can love God and love others.

One sad day, Tabitha became so sick that she died. When the other disciples heard Peter was close by, they sent two men to beg him to come quickly.

Peter went right away—he was ready and willing to help Tabitha.

The men brought Peter to the upstairs room where Tabitha was. There were women there crying. They were widows, and they showed Peter the clothing that Tabitha had made. Peter asked them all to leave the room. *What do you think Peter did next?*

Peter knelt and prayed. He turned to Tabitha and said, "Tabitha, get up." And immediately, Tabitha opened her eyes and sat up. Peter took Tabitha's hand and helped her stand. Then he called everyone into the room to see the miracle that had just happened: Tabitha was alive again! *How do you think they reacted when they saw their close friend Tabitha alive and well?* The news about Tabitha became known all over town. And many people put their faith in Jesus.

? QUESTIONS

- What did Peter do right before healing Tabitha?
- Why do you think Tabitha spent her time helping the poor?
- What is beautiful about Tabitha's heart?

PRAYER

Father, please help us to give and love like Tabitha did. Open our eyes to see people in need so we can help them and join in Your Kingdom work. In Jesus' name, amen.

 DAUGHTERS IN ACTION

Materials: Items to give away

Gather clothes and toys to give away to a shelter or a family in need. Some places where you can donate items are homeless shelters, foster care group homes, or foster care closets that give clothes to families who foster children. To make it more fun, play some music while gathering the items and bagging them up to give away.

 CREATIVE FUN

Materials: Pictures, painter's tape

Create a prayer wall in your home with pictures of people you want to pray for. You can use painter's tape to affix the pictures to the wall. Another idea is to decorate a poster board with the photos and write the names of the family and friends you've committed to pray for. Pray together often for these people, and rejoice in times of answered prayer!

36

PRAISE, BAPTISM, AND HOSPITALITY—LYDIA

(Acts 16)

Words for Your Heart

Be hospitable to one another without complaining. Based on the gift each one has received, use it to serve others.

I PETER 4:9-10

*P*aul and Silas were missionaries for Jesus, which means they shared about Jesus with others. They traveled together to tell people about the Lord, and they also encouraged those who had formed the churches. One of the places they sailed to was Macedonia. *If you sailed with Paul and could only bring three items, what would you bring?*

When they landed in Macedonia, they went to the town of Philippi. During that time, there were often places of prayer by the riverside where people who believed in God met to pray. On the Sabbath day, Paul and Silas went outside the city gate to one of the places of prayer. They sat down and spoke to the women there.

One of the women was Lydia. She sold expensive purple cloth. She was a Gentile. Gentiles were people who were not Jewish. Often they didn't believe in God. But Lydia believed in the one true God and worshipped Him. *Even though Lydia had a business selling cloth, what did she still make time to do?* Lydia was probably a busy woman, but she still made time to worship the Lord. *How do you worship the Lord?* We know that Lydia worshipped through prayer. Some other ways to worship God are through singing, reading the Bible, and serving others.

As Lydia sat listening to Paul and Silas, the Lord opened her heart to Paul's message about Jesus so she could understand it. When we take time to pray and listen to God, our hearts are more open to hear and connect with Him.

Lydia and everyone in her home were baptized—what a celebration that must have been! After the baptisms, Lydia invited Paul and Silas to stay at her home. She was hospitable and took care of their needs. *What is a way you can be hospitable, or welcoming, when someone visits?*

Later on, Paul and Silas were on their way to the place of prayer again. Some people in the town said that Paul and Silas were teaching wrong things, but they were teaching the truth about Jesus. The people complained to the city officials, and Paul and Silas were arrested.

The officers took Paul and Silas to jail and locked their feet in chains. In the middle of the night, Paul and Silas prayed and sang hymns to God. *How do you think God felt about that?* The other prisoners listened to Paul and Silas praying and singing to God. Suddenly, a violent earthquake shook the foundations of the prison. At once, all the prison doors flew open and everybody's chains came loose!

The jailer rushed in and fell trembling before Paul and Silas and asked, "What must I do to be saved?" *What do you think they told him?* They said, "Believe in Jesus and you will be saved." Then Paul and Silas told the jailer and everyone in his house more about Jesus. The jailer took care of Paul and Silas. He washed their wounds and fed them a good meal. On that very day, the jailer and his whole family were baptized. And they were joyful because of their belief in God.

As soon as it was daylight, Paul and Silas were released from prison. *Where do you think they went?* They went back to Lydia's house. She opened up her home to support her friends and to have a place to worship God together. Paul and Silas continued encouraging believers in Lydia's home.

? QUESTIONS

- What are some ways Lydia showed her love for God?
- Just as Lydia hosted Paul, Silas, and other friends, who would you like to invite over to have fellowship with?
- What is beautiful about Lydia's heart?

✠ PRAYER

Lord, I pray we would have open hearts to You, like Lydia did. And just as she was hospitable and welcomed others into her home to encourage them, help us do the same. In Jesus' name, amen.

⌘ DAUGHTERS IN ACTION

Invite a family over for fellowship and encouragement. Be hospitable like Lydia was by preparing for their visit. During their visit, you could ask someone to share his or her baptism or faith story. If you have a meal together, you could also write imaginative, thoughtful, or silly questions on note cards and put one or two under each napkin. During the meal, each person can answer his or her question(s) to get to know one another better. You can find a list of hilarious "Would You Rather" questions to ask in Appendix B (pg. 184).

CREATIVE FUN

Materials: Two small treats, a blindfold

This activity encourages having open ears like Lydia's. Hide a treat or any small item. Then blindfold your daughter with a scarf. Direct her toward the surprise by saying the direction and number of steps to walk. Tell her to listen closely so she can find it. Then switch roles. Have your daughter put a blindfold on you, hide something, and then direct you to it.

37

STANDING OUT FROM THE CROWD—DAMARIS

(Acts 17)

Words for Your Heart

You will seek Me and find Me when
you search for Me with all your heart.

JEREMIAH 29:13

$\mathcal{P}$aul continued visiting many places to share about Jesus. One place he traveled to was Athens, Greece. He was distressed because the city worshipped so many idols instead of the one true God. In hopes that they would change, Paul told them about Jesus and how He rose from the dead. *How do you think people responded to Paul's message?*

Some people made fun of Paul when he talked about Jesus. *Do you think Paul stopped preaching because of people teasing him?* Paul wanted to please the Lord more than people, so he kept on preaching. Paul knew that the people in the crowd needed to know the truth about Jesus. And Paul knew that some of the people would hear the truth and believe it. *If you were standing in the crowd listening to Paul, what do you think you would have done?*

There was a woman in the crowd named Damaris. She heard Paul's words and chose to believe in Jesus, along with many others. Damaris didn't follow the people making fun of Paul because she cared more about seeking and knowing the Lord.

Other people in the crowd weren't sure what they believed yet and asked Paul to come back later. But Damaris didn't wait to decide. As she stood in the crowd, regardless of what other people did, she chose faith in Jesus, then and there. She had an open heart to hear the message, and she believed.

God knew Damaris would be in the crowd that day. He cared deeply about her and wanted her to believe in Him. While the Lord longs for everyone to come to Him, He is a God of love and doesn't force anyone. *How do you think the Lord felt when Damaris chose to have faith and believe in Jesus in that moment?*

Just as the Lord knew Damaris would be in the crowd that day, learning about Him and seeking Him, the Lord also knows that you're reading this devotional right now, learning more about Him. It pleases the Lord so much when you seek Him. God promises us that when we seek Him with all of our heart, we will find Him.

What a beautiful promise that when we believe in Jesus like Damaris did, the Lord will be with us now and forever. *Nothing* will ever separate us from Jesus' awesome love.

❓ QUESTIONS

- What do you think helped Damaris focus on God instead of the crowd's insults and teasing?
- How did Damaris show her love for God?
- What is beautiful about Damaris' heart?

PRAYER

Lord, we're thankful that Damaris chose to seek You and believe in You that day in the crowd. I pray we would also have confidence and faith in You, no matter what people around us choose to do. In Jesus' name, amen.

 DAUGHTERS IN ACTION

Materials: Note cards, pens or markers

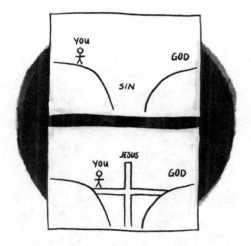

Paul shared the Good News with Damaris, and she believed. You and your daughter can create this illustration to share the Good News with someone. Each of you will need a note card. On one side of the note cards, draw the top illustration on this page. Practice explaining that all people sin and fall short of God's perfection and glory. Our sin separates us from God.

On the other side of the note cards, draw the bottom illustration. Practice explaining that because Jesus loves us so much, He took our sins upon Him when He died on the Cross even though He lived a perfect life. Then He rose again on the third day. Jesus' death and resurrection provide a way for us to be with God. When we put our faith in what Jesus did for us, we can be with Him now and forever!

Then keep your note cards in a handy place. If a conversation about Jesus comes up with friends, you can pull out your note card to explain what Jesus did for us because of His awesome love.

 CREATIVE FUN

Materials: Cardstock, crayons or markers, scissors, brad fasteners, glue

Damaris was a courageous woman who chose to seek and follow God, regardless of what the people around her were doing.

With your daughter, create a large paper doll from cardstock of Damaris or yourself. Since the Bible doesn't describe what she looked like, you'll need to use your imagination if you make a doll of Damaris. Use brad fasteners for the arms and legs so that they move. Glue a speech bubble coming from her mouth that says: "The God who made the world and everything in it—He is Lord of heaven and earth" (Acts 17:24). Then hang it on the wall to be reminded of what Damaris learned from Paul that day.

38

SAILING THE SEAS
—PRISCILLA

(Acts 18, Romans 16)

Words for Your Heart

Everyone should look out not only for his own interests,
but also for the interests of others.

PHILIPPIANS 2:4

*A*fter leaving Athens, Paul went to Corinth. He met a woman there named Priscilla (also known as Prisca), and her husband, Aquila. They had just come from Rome because Claudius, the ruler there, had ordered all the Jews to leave.

Paul stayed in Corinth and worked with Priscilla and Aquila. There was a certain item that Priscilla, Aquila, and Paul made and sold to earn money. *Can you guess what it was?* I'll give you a clue: You can sleep in these outside. . . . They made tents! *If you could make anything, what would you want to make?*

Priscilla, Aquila, and Paul were believers who encouraged one another and worked together to spread the Gospel of Jesus. Though some people didn't believe their message about Jesus, many of the Corinthians believed and were baptized.

After some time in Corinth, Paul, Priscilla, and Aquila sailed away together on a boat. *Why do you think they sailed to other places together to tell people about Jesus?* They got off the boat in Ephesus, and Paul went to the synagogue. Some of the people asked Paul to spend more time with them, but he said, "I will come back if it is God's will." It was important to Paul to listen to God first. Paul continued sailing from place to place, teaching and encouraging those who believed in Jesus. *If you could sail anywhere in the world, where would you want to sail?*

Meanwhile, Priscilla and Aquila stayed in Ephesus and taught people about God. This showed how deeply they cared for others—they took time to teach them about Jesus. They met a smart man named Apollos who was passionate about the Scriptures. He knew the Old Testament Scriptures very well, and he knew much about Jesus, too. But there were some things he didn't fully understand. Priscilla invited Apollos to their home and taught him more about the Lord.

After some time, Priscilla and Aquila could finally return to Rome. Paul wrote a letter to believers there asking that they welcome his friends. In the letter, Paul shared that Priscilla and Aquila followed Jesus, had supported many churches, and that one of the churches even met in their home. Paul also let the Roman believers know that Priscilla and Aquila had risked their lives for him. *How do you think they might have risked their lives for Paul?*

❓ QUESTIONS

- How did Priscilla and Aquila show Apollos they cared about him?
- Who would you like to teach about Jesus? Which Bible passage would you want to share?
- What is beautiful about Priscilla's heart?

✝ PRAYER

Lord, we are thankful that Priscilla took time to teach people about You. Please help us to take time to teach others about You. In Jesus' name, amen.

🔖 DAUGHTERS IN ACTION

Just as Priscilla taught Apollos more about Jesus, share a story about Jesus' life with others. You could share the passage with people at church, with your parents, a sibling, a friend, or a grandparent.

CREATIVE FUN

Materials: bedsheets, chairs

As Priscilla, Aquila, and Paul were making tents together, they probably talked about Jesus and shared about Him with one another. Create a tent in your living room using sheets and chairs, or set up a real tent! Share some of your treasured family memories and favorite Bible passages about Jesus. To make the time even more fun, make some yummy s'mores to share!

39

A SERVANT LEADER —PHOEBE

(Romans 16)

Words for Your Heart

Serve one another through love.

GALATIANS 5:13

$\mathcal{P}$aul loved encouraging people in the Lord and teaching them about Jesus. One important way that Paul taught others was by writing letters. Remember there were no phones back then, so Paul couldn't call them or send a quick text to encourage someone.

Paul wanted to connect with the people of Rome, so he wrote a letter to them. We can read the letter that Paul wrote to them— it's the book of Romans in the Bible. At the end of his letter, he sends lots of greetings to the people there and sends information to the people to help them get to know one another better. One person Paul mentions in his letter is a woman named Phoebe.

Paul tells the believers in Rome that Phoebe is coming to them. Paul asks the believers to make her feel welcome. *How can you make a new kid feel welcome at your church, school, or at an event?*

Paul called Phoebe "our sister." *Why do you think he called her "sister" if she wasn't his actual sister?* God is our Father, and all who believe in Him are His children, so Christians sometimes call fellow believers "brothers and sisters in Christ." It's similar to being such close friends with people that you consider them family.

Phoebe had been a great helper and leader at the church in Cenchreae. Great leaders care about others and serve them out of love. Phoebe was a servant-hearted leader in her church.

Jesus tells us in Matthew 6:1 to be careful not to do good deeds in front of others to be seen by them. *Why do you think the Lord doesn't want us to be showy when we do good things, but to be humble?* The Lord wants us to serve Him and others, like Phoebe did, out of love for them and not for attention.

Paul asked the believers in Rome to help Phoebe with anything she needed because she had been such a great help to so many people, including him. *In what ways do you think Phoebe might have helped Paul and others?*

Tryphaena, Tryphosa, and Persis were three other women Paul greeted in Rome. He said that they had worked hard for God. *Why do you think these followers of Jesus worked together?* One of the great purposes the Lord had for these women was helping and supporting other believers.

Phoebe and the other women followed Paul's words: "Serve one another through love." Serving and helping can be hard if we're only doing it because we have to. But if we help others because we care about them, God's love will shine through us. *How can you show your family you're helping them, not because you have to, but because you love them?*

? QUESTIONS

- How can you be a servant-hearted leader at church, at school, or with your friends?

- Who is someone you think of as a great helper like Phoebe? How can you help that person?
- What is beautiful about Phoebe's heart?

 PRAYER

Lord, help us to be servant leaders like Phoebe. We want to help those around us out of love for them. Please fill our hearts with your love so it will overflow to others. Thank You, Lord. In Jesus' name, amen.

 DAUGHTERS IN ACTION

Materials: Piece of wood, canvas, or tile; a paint pen

Find a piece of wood, canvas, or tile in your house to paint or get one at a craft store. Use a paint pen or paintbrush to decorate it. Write Galatians 5:13 on it: "Serve one another through love." Display it as a reminder to serve others out of love for them and the Lord.

 CREATIVE FUN

"Backward Day" is a fun way to reinforce what it's like to be a servant-hearted leader. While a great leader might be thought of as a person who just orders other people around, it's actually backward from that—a great leader is someone who leads by example and serves others.

Your daughter can practice being a servant leader by doing everything backward for a day. Support your daughter as she takes over some of the leadership tasks you usually do in your home.

Then add some silliness to it and do the whole day backward. For example:

- In the morning, make sure your daughter doesn't make her bed!

- Have dessert for breakfast along with food you'd normally have for dinner.
- Then prepare breakfast foods at dinnertime.
- Instead of getting dressed that day, your daughter could stay in her pajamas and then put regular clothes on at night to sleep in!
- Your daughter could make her bed just before going to sleep. She could sleep on top of her made bed with a sleeping bag. Join in the fun and grab your sleeping bag, too, to have a bedroom campout together!

Think of as many silly ideas as you can for Backward Day!

40

LEAVING A LEGACY
—LOIS AND EUNICE

(2 Timothy 1)

Words for Your Heart

We will tell the next generation the praiseworthy deeds of the LORD,
his power, and the wonders he has done.

PSALM 78:4, NIV

What is one way your mom or grandma is beautiful hearted? Lois
was a woman in the Bible who was beautiful hearted and had great
faith. Her daughter Eunice also came to know God and had a deep
faith in Him.

Eunice had a son named Timothy. He learned about God from
his mom, Eunice, and his grandmother Lois. At that time, Lois
and Eunice didn't know that when Timothy was older, he would
be taught by Paul, a great Christian missionary. Two books in the
Bible, 1 Timothy and 2 Timothy, are letters that Paul wrote to
Timothy.

Lois and Eunice also didn't know that one day Timothy would
be the pastor of the church of Ephesus and a great leader for Jesus.
But because Lois and Eunice were faithful to teach Timothy about

the Lord, he was prepared to learn from Paul. Paul even called Timothy his "son in the faith." And many people became believers because of Timothy.

Even though you're a young girl, you can also be a follower of Jesus who makes a difference in the world now and when you're older. The Lord cares about everything you do for Him, whether small or big.

When you choose to include a kid who's left out, God sees.

When you share a Bible verse with someone who's hurting, God notices.

When you forgive your sibling even though it's hard, God knows.

When you read the Bible to know God better, God notices.

When you listen to your parents, God sees.

When you ask for forgiveness after you hurt someone, God knows.

When you praise the Lord or ask Him for help, God hears.

When everyone is doing the wrong thing, but you choose to do the right thing because of your love for Jesus, God knows and is honored. *How are you making a difference for Jesus—whether it's a way you have loved someone or a time you've told someone about the Lord?*

Lois and Eunice made a great difference for the Lord by taking time to learn about God and teach Timothy about Him. You've been learning about God through this devotional. *What is something you've learned about the Lord during these devotional times?*

Simply reading this devotional might seem small in your eyes, but it's a big way to show love for God. It's a way to grow a beautiful heart and become like the women of the Bible we've learned about. *If you could be one of these women of the Bible for a day, which one would you want to be?*

Lois and Eunice taught Timothy about the Lord, one day at a

time, one moment at a time, one verse at a time. They loved each other, and they loved Timothy. *What is one big or small way your mom has loved you well? And, Mom, what is one way you have felt loved by your daughter?*

Lois and Eunice were a beautiful hearted mother and daughter from long ago who left a legacy of love, faith, and devotion that we still hear about today. You can also leave a legacy of being a beautiful hearted mother and daughter by loving God and others, one moment at a time.

? QUESTIONS

- How did Lois and Eunice help Timothy grow in his faith?
- What is one way you can leave a legacy of loving Jesus and others?
- What is beautiful about Lois's and Eunice's hearts?

✚ PRAYER

Lord, help us seek You daily and love You and others with all our hearts, just like Lois and Eunice did, one moment at a time. In Jesus' name, amen.

⌦ DAUGHTERS IN ACTION

Materials: 1 cup very warm water, 1 tablespoon granulated sugar, 2 tablespoons dish soap, a straw for each person

Lois and Eunice taught Timothy about God when he was young, and later he taught many other people about Jesus. This bubble activity is a fun extension on leaving a legacy like Lois and Eunice did. As you make bubbles inside of other bubbles, think about how sharing the love of the Lord with those around us can lead to generations and generations of beautiful hearted mothers and daughters who love the Lord and one another with all their hearts.

1. Mix all ingredients together until the sugar dissolves, but don't overmix it because it shouldn't be foamy.

2. Cover a large, smooth surface that can get wet with some of the bubble solution. If the bubble touches the part that is not wet, it will pop.

3. Dip one end of the straw into the solution. Take the straw out and blow a large bubble onto the surface.

4. Then take the straw out of the bubble and dip it into the solution again. Put the wet end of the straw a few inches into the large bubble and gently blow another bubble inside that one. As long as there is bubble solution on the part of the straw that touches the large bubble, it won't pop. Continue this process and blow as many bubbles as you can inside the other bubbles until they pop!

CREATIVE FUN

Materials: Praise music, ingredients to make pancakes, griddle, spatula, chocolate chips

Celebrate completing this devotional book with a pancake feast!

1. Turn up some praise music. This is a great way to worship God!

2. Make the batter for your favorite pancakes. Add red food coloring if you'd like.

3. Pour the batter onto the griddle in heart shapes as a reminder

of God's greatest commandments: to love God and love others.

4. Add some chocolate chips for extra deliciousness. Then flip the pancakes.

5. As you enjoy eating the pancakes, talk about which woman of the Bible was your favorite and why.

6. Now that you have learned about so many beautiful hearted women of the Bible who left legacies of loving God and others, see how many you can name. Ready, set, go!

Jesus' Birth "Chain Links," Devotion 21

12. Mary was engaged to Joseph, and they would soon be married! (What do you imagine their wedding was like?)

11. Gabriel the angel appeared to Mary in Nazareth announcing, "Greetings! The Lord has blessed you! The Lord is with you." (How do you think Mary felt after hearing that the Lord was with her?)

10. Mary was scared when she saw the angel, but he said, "Don't be afraid, Mary. God is pleased with you." (Why didn't Mary need to be afraid?)

9. The angel said, "You will soon give birth to a son who is to be named Jesus." (*Jesus* means "savior.") "Nothing is impossible with God." (Why do you think the Son of God is named Jesus?)

8. Mary knew it was an honor to carry God's Son and said, "I am God's servant. May it happen just as you've said." (How did Mary put God first?)

7. Mary hurried to Elizabeth's home and shared the exciting news. Mary said, "God has done great things for me—His name is holy." (How did Mary show her gratefulness to the Lord for being chosen to have Jesus?)

6. Mary and Elizabeth celebrated together. Elizabeth was to have a son, even though she was older. And Mary would have a child who would be the Messiah. (What is one way you think they celebrated together?)

5. Later, Mary and Joseph traveled to Bethlehem for the Roman census. (Think about what you do on road trips to stay busy—Joseph and Mary's trip would have taken days, so what do you think they did along the way?)

4. Once Mary and Joseph arrived in Bethlehem, they were tired from the long trip. They searched for a place to rest so Mary could have her baby. (We're getting closer to Jesus' birthday! Hooray! How do you think Mary was feeling at this point?)

3. They searched for a place to stay, but there weren't enough rooms in the inns. Jesus would soon be coming. They had to find a place quickly. (Do you remember how God provided a place for them to stay?)

2. They finally found a stable to stay in. Mary would soon have Jesus. (What animals do you think might have been there on Jesus' birthday?)

1. Jesus was born! Mary wrapped Him in strips of cloth and placed Him in the manger. Jesus was also called Immanuel, which means "God with us." God loved us so much that He came to earth to be with us. (What is one way you can celebrate Jesus' birthday?)

Fifteen "Would You Rather" Questions, Devotion 36

Would you rather . . .

1. Never brush your teeth again or never take a bath again?

2. Have stinky feet or stinky hands?

3. Crawl everywhere or walk in a handstand everywhere?

4. Not wash your hands or not wash your hair for a month?

5. Eat a chocolate-covered cricket or a chocolate-covered worm?

6. Have five noses or five eyes?

7. Sleep on pinecones or spaghetti?

8. Be smaller than an ant or bigger than a tree?

9. Have feet on your head or hands on your knees?

10. Have noodles or broccoli for hair?

11. Be sprayed by a snail's slime or a spider's web?

12. Have an elephant's trunk or a giraffe's neck?

13. Be able to shoot slime or chocolate out of your fingertips?

14. Live on a cloud or at the bottom of the sea?

15. Be able to be invisible or fly whenever you want?

Acknowledgments

Thank you to my husband, Christian, for your unconditional love and always being by my side; to my kids, Bates, Brooklyn, and Gracie, for simply being you and always cheering me on; to my dad for showing me that the heart matters most; to my mom for showing me how to be a loving mother; to all my family and friends for your unending support; and to Dave and Brian at WTA Media and Focus on the Family for believing in me and in this devotional.